EBURY PRESS
THE TIGER'S PAUSE

Swami Virupaksha, a transformative practice specialist, has dedicated his life to supporting and promoting the vision and mission of world-renowned spiritual leader Gurudev Sri Sri Ravi Shankar.

Besides Europe and India, Swami Virupaksha served in Sri Lanka for nine years as a key member of Gurudev's conflict-resolution team during and after the country's war-torn days.

Over the past twenty-two years, Swami Virupaksha has worked on delivering humanitarian initiatives that served all sections of society.

In training lawmakers, heads of state, the clergy, a national cricket team, war refugees, educationists, college students, prison inmates and corporates, he has brought people together in the spirit of voluntary service.

Born Vidyut Udiaver, Swami Virupaksha is an alumnus of Don Bosco School and Loyola College, Chennai. He holds a degree in economics and business management. He has experience in brand management, having worked in leading international marketing and advertising firms, including Ogilvy & Mather (O&M) and L'Oréal.

He is an aficionado of art, music, languages and world culture, and his love for French, creativity and moments of deep silence make him feel at home wherever he goes.

Currently based in Bangalore, he is also an advanced meditation teacher with the Art of Living global movement.

ADVANCE PRAISE FOR THE BOOK

'Great leaders put grit, determination and duty first, before personal comfort. Gurudev Sri Sri Ravi Shankar risked his life, putting everything at stake, even though he was made to walk through dangerous landmine-studded paths, to save the future of thousands of people in war-torn Sri Lanka. This is the measure of a true peacemaker. *The Tiger's Pause* reflects the essence of Gurudev, making the book unputdownable'—Dr Kiran Bedi, twenty-fourth lieutenant governor of Puducherry and IPS (retired)

'The author's narration is very interesting and informative. Having dealt with the Sri Lankan Tamil crisis myself, while investigating the assassination of former prime minister Rajiv Gandhi, I can very well appreciate the various situations and episodes in *The Tiger's Pause*. If only the rebel Tamil leadership had listened to the wise counsel of Gurudev Sri Sri Ravi Shankar, history would have been very different and hundreds of thousands of innocent Tamil lives could have been saved. It is unfortunate that such a peaceful resolution of the ethnic conflict in Sri Lanka could not take place'—D.R. Kaarthikeyan, IPS; former director, CBI; DG, CRPF; DG, NHRC; and chief of the special investigation team of the CBI that successfully investigated the Rajiv Gandhi assassination case

'This book showcases Gurudev's "spirit of responsibility" towards making a difference in the lives of a nation and its people'—Juan Carlos Losada, member of Parliament, Colombia

'Sri Sri Ravi Shankar is teaching millions of individuals to pursue inner peace, and to love their friends and family. This book illuminates another aspect of his unique practice: helping communities manage their differences and live in peace. Swami Virupaksha provides a unique insight into Sri Sri Ravi Shankar's effort to promote peace in Sri Lanka for over a decade. In a world in disarray, we can learn about a millennial Indian tradition to reduce conflicts. Technological innovations are increasing humanity's ability to kill and fight, and this book offers a unique possibility to learn from reality on how to coexist. The activities of Sri Sri Ravi Shankar that have been described in the book should be transformed into educational material for individuals, diplomats and whoever aspires to establish peace in humanity'—Luis Moreno Ocampo, first prosecutor, International Criminal Court, The Hague, the Netherlands

THE TIGER'S PAUSE

The Untold Story of
Gurudev Sri Sri Ravi Shankar's
Peace Efforts in Sri Lanka

SWAMI VIRUPAKSHA

EBURY
PRESS

An imprint of Penguin Random House

EBURY PRESS

USA | Canada | UK | Ireland | Australia
New Zealand | India | South Africa | China

Ebury Press is part of the Penguin Random House group of companies
whose addresses can be found at global.penguinrandomhouse.com

Published by Penguin Random House India Pvt. Ltd
4th Floor, Capital Tower 1, MG Road,
Gurugram 122 002, Haryana, India

Penguin
Random House
India

First published in Ebury Press by Penguin Random House India 2022

10 9 8 7 6 5 4 3 2 1

This book is a work of non-fiction. The views and opinions expressed in the book
are those of the author only and do not reflect or represent the views and opinions
held by any other person.
This book is based on a variety of sources including published materials, research,
experiences of the author, and his interactions with the persons mentioned in the
manuscript. It reflects the author's own understanding and conception of such
materials.
The objective of this book is not to hurt any sentiments or be biased in favour
of or against any particular person, political party, region, caste, society, gender,
creed, nation or religion.

ISBN 9780143456988

The names of many characters have been changed to protect their identity.

Typeset in Adobe Garamond Pro by Manipal Technologies Limited, Manipal

www.penguin.co.in

To my spiritual master, Gurudev Sri Sri Ravi Shankar, who taught me the fine art and skill to pause in meditation before 'I leap' into the jungle safari of life, almost every day. His inspiration led me to taste and experience the highest knowledge towards realizing my potential.

To the thousands of Art of Living teachers and millions of volunteers around the world, who are working to spread wisdom, peace and happiness.

To my parents, who encouraged me to discover the mystical, relaxed enigma that is Gurudev.

Contents

Contents

Preface

Sri Lanka, the beautiful island nation nestled in the Indian Ocean around 30 km from India's southernmost point of Rameswaram, gained freedom from the British in 1948. But tensions were growing even before the British left.

A section of the Sinhala-speaking Buddhist majority, the Sinhalese, resented the colonial era British favouritism towards the Tamil minority. The Sinhalese felt that they had been treated unfairly, getting the short end of the stick, thus reducing their socio-economic opportunities.

This resentment was just one of the seeds of ethnic tension between the Sinhalese and the Tamils that culminated in one of Asia's longest civil wars from July 1983 to May 2009.

Post-independence, several other causes widened the ethnic divide in Sri Lanka. Tamil plantation workers who had migrated from India felt deprived of their rights, Sinhala was made the official language and Buddhism was declared the primary religion. Then came the Bandaranaike-Chelvanayakam Pact of 1957 that seemed to signal a certain level of autonomy for the Tamil population. However, the agreement was abandoned in less than a year. All these events and decisions, especially the discontinuation of the pact, led to ethnic violence between the two communities, eventually culminating in Sri Lanka's nearly three-decade-long civil war.

The last straw was the standardization policy in the education system that marginalized the Tamil youth. In 1971, a system of standardization of marks was introduced for university admissions to curtail the number of Tamil students selected for certain faculties in varsities. Though the policy was annulled in 1977, this issue became the focal point of the conflict between the government and Tamil leaders. Embittered by this discrimination and inspired by different schools of thought, the Tamil youth had already started forming various political groups since the early 1970s. This is a lesson in how policies and insensitivity towards minority interests can exacerbate ethnic tensions.

These events inspired a young Velupillai Prabhakaran to relaunch his youth group, Tamil New Tigers, and lead an armed movement in 1976 known as the Liberation Tigers of Tamil Eelam or the LTTE (popularly called the Tamil Tigers). This movement slowly eclipsed other non-violent and radical Tamil groups of the time.

Prabhakaran stated that he chose military measures only after observing that non-violent means were ineffectual and obsolete.

The LTTE vigorously campaigned for a separate Tamil homeland, called Tamil Eelam, comprising all parts of north and east Sri Lanka. These areas are where most Tamils reside to this day. Prabhakaran's campaign found widespread acceptance and support from Indian Tamils in Tamil Nadu.

Tamil-speaking Sri Lankans comprised the rank and file of the LTTE, which broadened the scope and operations of its movement to become one of the deadliest guerrilla groups in history.

On the night of 23 July 1983, the LTTE rose to prominence by ambushing and killing thirteen soldiers from the Sri Lankan army. This led to a ruthless and retaliatory massacre of Tamils across the island. Mobs looted and burned houses, shops and commercial establishments, killing several hundred Tamils and leaving many injured. Thousands fled the island and landed up on the shores of India as refugees.

Though Sri Lanka saw anti-Tamil riots in 1956, 1958, 1977 and 1981, these intermittent conflicts escalated into a full-scale nationalist insurgency. This, in a way, contributed to the start of the civil war in Sri Lanka from 1983 till 1987. Consecutive wars between the Government of Sri Lanka and the LTTE were fought in 1990–1995, 1995–2002 and 2006–2009.

In 2002, both parties accepted a Ceasefire Agreement (CFA) brokered by the Norwegians. This was followed by a brief respite in hostilities. However, the cycle of violence, assassinations and suicide bombings continued during the twenty-six-year war.

Many Sri Lankan Tamils who fled to India—their natural and initial destination considering the shared linguistic, religious and political affinities with the over 6 crore Tamils in Tamil Nadu—later on migrated to Western countries. This shaped the powerful Tamil community abroad, which began to wholeheartedly support the LTTE till the culmination of the war in the sweltering summer of 2009.

Successive Sri Lankan governments reached out to the LTTE with varied proposals and potential political solutions, which changed each time a new government was elected. Several rounds of peace talks and many attempts at reconciliation failed to yield results as deep mistrust on both sides led to yet another phase of deadly violence.

In the midst of all this violence, Gurudev Sri Sri Ravi Shankar, humanitarian and world-renowned spiritual leader from India, played a key role in offering support to the war-ravaged people of Sri Lanka.

The Tiger's Pause is a detailed account of our experiences in the island nation and Gurudev's many attempts to broker peace between the LTTE and the Lankan government.

This is the untold story of how Gurudev walked into the conflict with a singular aim: to help the citizens of Sri Lanka find inner peace amid the bloodshed and violence. The book offers an intimate account of the time spent trying to save the very soul of a nation.

1

Seeds of Hope

A few months into the millennial year, the loud ringing of bells and musicians playing celebrative tunes on the nadaswaram and thavil signified the auspicious nature of the event.

This beautiful temple all the way in Toronto, Canada, was a meeting place for many ethnic Tamils. They came here to share, socialize, celebrate, catch up on gossip, but, above all, pray to the presiding deity who represented valour, beauty and chivalry. Particularly for the Sri Lankan Tamils, this temple was the altar to resolve collective challenges as a persecuted community.

A large majority of Tamils around the world venerate this deity with fervour and devotion.

That evening, the kids played around in their colourful best while the women wore the renowned Kanjeevaram sarees with intricately patterned borders made of golden thread.

Anandam kept looking at his watch every few minutes, occasionally gazing towards the temple gate. He was one of many who, during the 1983 riots, had fled from Sri Lanka as a young adult.

'What time is he expected?' he asked Karthik, who was standing there with his friends and discussing the violent situation back home in Sri Lanka.

Karthik reminded Anandam that this was the third time he was asking that question. Another man interjected, 'What's troubling you, Andy . . . is everything all right?'

Anandam ignored them and rushed to the temple kitchen to check if all the arrangements were on track. His role in the celebration was to ensure that the dinner packets were ready for the evening.

He returned to the temple gate and waited there impatiently.

The temple reception committee members reached the gate at 5 p.m. Anandam didn't bother with them and kept his gaze trained at the entrance in anticipation.

'Where is Saravana? I don't see him,' asked Karthik.

'He had a massive argument with his father at breakfast today,' mumbled Anandam. He went on to tell Karthik how Saravana's father was reading a Tamil Eelam publication and talking about the war when Saravana lost his cool.

'He snatched the paper from his father's hand, tore it to pieces and screamed about how Sri Lanka and the war had nothing to do with him and that it was the story of the older generation,' said Anandam, 'It was almost like a war at Saravana's house.'

'I was born in Canada and this is my country,' Saravana had yelled, throwing his coffee mug on the floor.

His angry father, a diehard Liberation Tigers of Tamil Eelam (LTTE) sympathizer, retorted, 'But our identity is Tamil. We are Tamils first . . . remember that. You have picked up the culture of chewing gum, jeans and leather jackets in this country.'

Saravana left in a huff. He stomped off to his bedroom, where he sat on his bed and covered his sweaty face.

His father stood at the door, 'We were chased away from our Tamil homeland and came to Toronto with absolutely nothing . . . we slogged at fuel stations, did babysitting, cleaned toilets, shovelled snow and did plumbing jobs . . . when you were just in your nappies. Don't you dare teach me what is right and wrong,'

Shalini quietly shut her son's bedroom door and pulled her husband away.

'Look there,' said Anandam, 'Shalini has come to the temple with her younger son. At least he respects our Tamil identity, though he's only two years younger than Saravana.'

Just then, a convoy of cars arrived and Anandam saw Gurudev for the first time. Karthik and Anandam had just completed the Art of Living programme and become thick friends. They were eagerly waiting to meet the man who had designed the programme they had enjoyed so thoroughly.

Amid loud music and chanting by priests, Gurudev stepped out of the vehicle. Anandam couldn't take his eyes off the man or his white robes that sparkled softly, just like his beatific smile.

'One needs to see him to believe him,' whispered Anandam to Karthik. The waiting crowd surged forward. Anandam made his way to the front and offered a huge bouquet of red and yellow roses to Gurudev saying, 'Welcome to our temple.'

Anandam had specifically ordered that bouquet; the red and yellow roses signified the colours of the LTTE and their Tamil Eelam nation. Perhaps this gesture telegraphed Anandam's intention of handing over the insurmountable challenges of the Tamils to Gurudev. An article of personal faith for him.

Karthik played his role of draping the ponnadai, a dazzling shawl, around Gurudev's shoulders.

White lilies and chrysanthemums adorned the pathway, where a procession of temple priests walked after welcoming Gurudev with the poorna kumbham, the sacred pot.

All these gestures constitute a traditional welcome in the Indian subcontinent for an honoured guest.

'He has a powerful yet peaceful presence,' said Karthik.

The deities at the temple were now honoured with incense sticks and lamps of various shapes and sizes, while Gurudev stood with his eyes closed in prayer. Drumbeats reverberated and bells chimed vigorously. Gurudev was then led to the adjoining hall, where young Tamil adults and children, who had only known this Canadian temple, sat with their parents and elders who grew up on Sri Lankan soil.

Two generations with different needs and aspirations jostled for space in that hall.

The children swiftly broke into a cultural dance portraying the essence of the journey of devotion. Celebrating their performance, Gurudev offered chocolates to the twenty-odd kids and spoke about the essence of meditation and its practical relevance in daily life.

A man in green combat fatigues, a former LTTE operative, stood up to speak. 'Our relatives in Sri Lanka are struggling with their lives for many years. We have shown great valour, won battles against the Sinhalese military. What can you do for us?' He had apparently worn that uniform to highlight the unresolved Tamil issue.

His elderly aunt chimed in, 'We left everything there as we ran out of our homes to get into boats and run away to India. They robbed all my jewellery, snatched away my wedding ring and necklace, burnt my house in Point Pedro right in front of my eyes . . . the Sri Lankan army.'

She cried loudly, 'Will we ever get back our homes . . . our peace?'

Gurudev listened to many more such people voicing their plight, their emotions bursting through. They seemed shackled by their struggles and sorrows, seeing no hope for tomorrow.

Karthik's cousin asked, 'Are we Tamils to continue our armed liberation struggle or non-violence will bring us the solution? Till date it has not . . . Our lands, wealth, dignity have all been taken away by the oppressive Sinhalese government.'

Their suffering was palpable though they had worked hard and earned a living in Canada over the last two decades since their forced migration.

Gurudev replied, 'Yes . . . we can all work together to bring peace.'

Anandam shouted from the last row, 'How can we assist you? Please tell us.'

'We will discuss,' said Gurudev.

Satgunarajah and Sothy began to sing a beautiful Tamil devotional song, praising the powerful patron deity of courage and warfare.

The entire hall began to reverberate with 'Arohara Arohara', the traditional, sacred Tamil chant. Many danced in step with the beats of the drums, cymbals and conch shells.

Gurudev closed his eyes and started meditating.

A few minutes later, when people began to settle down after the hymn, Gajendran blew the conch shell once again. The shrill sound swirled up the spines of the audience, raising the sacred energy in the environment.

'Gurudev is bringing us a new beginning . . . we hope. Liberation will happen in our motherland . . . Tamil motherland,' said Anandam.

People cheered and clapped. The women wiped away their tears as they now saw a ray of hope in Gurudev.

'Let us meditate. Let's close our eyes,' Gurudev said into the microphone.

Twenty minutes later, Anandam asked for the big tub of sweet pongal to be brought in.

He offered the prasadam to everyone. The crowd began to proceed towards the entrance, where they were handed the dinner packets before they left for home.

Karthik, Anandam, Gurudev and a few others sat down in the temple hall. A long discussion ensued.

~

'That night was unforgettable,' said Karthik, as he recounted the entire story in detail to Swami Sadyojathah,* a senior teacher from the Art of Living, during his visit to the organization's ashram in Germany in the winter of 2000.

'But what did you discuss with Gurudev?' asked Swamiji.

Karthik laughed it off saying, 'Who knows . . . you may well become a part of all this.'

Christoph came running to Swamiji and said, 'Gurudev is calling you.' They rushed to his room.

'Tomorrow, some groups of Tamils are coming from Denmark, Norway, France and the UK. Make a programme for them. They will be here for about two days,' Gurudev told them.

Karthik and Swamiji rushed to the meditation hall and sat down to plan the programme, occasionally looking into the verdant expanse of the Black Forest right outside the giant glass windows.

'I had invited them all after taking Gurudev's approval,' said Karthik.

---

* Swami Sadyojathah is referred to as Swamiji in the book.

'They are all very keen and unanimous in their decision that Gurudev should help bring peace between the Tamils and the Sinhalese . . . a few are opposing the idea but that should not discourage us,' he said.

'Let us continue our peace work,' said Swamiji.

'There are a few who support continuing the military offensive till we achieve an independent Tamil nation,' Karthik said with a shrug.

'The LTTE has declared a unilateral ceasefire. The government of Sri Lanka is on a very weak wicket and will go for peace initiatives. This is the best time for Prabhakaran [the LTTE chief] to strengthen himself politically, militarily and economically. They have the upper hand militarily over many areas in the north and east,' added Karthik.

Swamiji quietly looked outside the window. It was snowing heavily. It looked like it was going to be a white Christmas and Gurudev was to deliver wisdom for the new millennium.

2

Tsunami in a Teacup

'Ladies and gentlemen, this is your captain speaking. Hope you are enjoying the flight to Colombo.'

I was definitely enjoying my flight, thanks to the string hoppers, fresh coconut sambol, and finely sliced mangoes and papaya on my breakfast plate.

For a moment, I looked outside the window and saw that we were crossing the famous Ram Setu bridge. The tide was low and we could see the beautiful, ancient marvel stand up against the mighty blue waters, steadfast for several centuries now.

The stunning blue waters gave way to fields and hills draped in lively green. For a moment, I wondered whether Kerala, God's own country, had a twin across the seas in Lanka.

The pilot had just brought that to our attention on this 31 December 2004 flight, when a tsunami had struck just a week earlier, leaving thousands of people dead. This was one New Year's Eve that the southern part of India and large parts of Sri Lanka were not celebrating. As though the death and destruction already caused by the lengthy civil war between the LTTE and the Lankan military was not enough.

An elderly Sinhalese co-passenger asked me if this was my first trip to Sri Lanka. In one way it was, but from another angle it wasn't.

I told him that I had had an overnight layover in Colombo in June 1994 while on the way to Singapore to visit my sister.

Flights to Singapore via Colombo were really affordable in those days and you got to experience two scenic island nations in one trip!

'That was a late-night flight so I couldn't see the Ram Setu bridge but I had a very bad welcome at your airport,' I told him regretfully.

'Oh really . . . what happened?' The man spilled the piping hot, world-famous Sri Lankan tea he was drinking. That wasn't an accidental slip; I saw that my anguish had touched his heart.

I told him how the visa officer at Colombo airport had blown his top without provocation. He had spat on the side and alleged that 'you bloody Indians come here to support the LTTE'. He had thrown the passport back in my face, only to seize it again and lock it up in his cupboard, so that I would not sneak into his country illegally. Though securing the passports of transit passengers leaving the airport premises was the accepted norm, the visa officer had obviously seen my Chennai address. Besides being the capital of Tamil Nadu in south India, Chennai was also the place where people actively supported Sri Lankan Tamils and the Tamil liberation movement. I protested and told the visa officer that I was only a transit passenger, but to no avail. The local tour operator comforted me with an apology and took me away for my scheduled overnight stay at a beautiful resort in Negombo.

When I returned to take my onward flight the following morning, I told the same visa officer, almost vengefully, 'One day, I *will* come back to your country.'

He sneered at me and threw my passport on the table. As the flight took off, I thought to myself that no wonder the Lankan Tamils had been crying for justice at the hands of the Sinhalese majority.

But I did not conclude that every Sinhala had the same attitude. Every society has its devil and deity.

In the early 1990s, the relations between India and Sri Lanka were at an all-time low given the unfortunate turn of events in both the countries: the assassination of Ranasinghe Premadasa, the famous Lankan president and the darling of the Sinhala masses, and Rajiv Gandhi, the former Indian prime minister, both by the LTTE.

~

I was on the threshold of graduating. My economics exams had just concluded and I was looking forward to pursuing my postgraduate studies in French.

My father thought otherwise and persuaded me to take up 'a more professional' line of study.

He told me as much that Tuesday noon during his phone call from the US, 'We can't have a French daughter-in-law!'

I just couldn't convince the globe-trotting sailor in my dad. Though he had travelled the world, his views were traditionally Indian in some respects.

A badminton game that evening was imperative to release my tension. The game was getting really exciting as I joined some friends to play in the car-park lane of our apartments.

Chetan came rushing towards us, 'Hey . . . come quickly . . . Let's go near Panagal Park. There's a huge crowd there.'

I asked him, 'What happened now?'

He replied, 'It seems Rajiv Gandhi is coming there.'

The nation was facing a general election and he was likely to be re-elected as the prime minister.

We ran on the road. In just under two minutes, we reached the junction near Ramakrishna Mission Boys School, a landmark that had been around for almost a century, opposite Chennai's famous Panagal Park, where people 'shop till they drop'.

I was now going to get a glimpse of another legend—the son of Indira Gandhi, the former prime minister.

Police personnel were blowing their whistles and stopping traffic at different points of that busy five-point junction. The crowd was light but the anticipation heavy. People were perhaps seeing Rajiv Gandhi for the first time. Just like my friends and me.

I left them behind in the crowd and found a vantage point.

In a few minutes the convoy arrived, led by a police jeep tooting its siren and followed by a motorcade.

A white Ambassador slowed down to negotiate a rather steep bend, when I suddenly spotted a young Rajiv Gandhi seated in the front passenger seat.

The window was rolled down. A yellow dome light inside the car amplified his 1000-watt smile as he waved at the people. I had never seen a national leader that close. That too, India's youngest prime minister. Mildly cherubic and blushing, with a certain warmth in his eyes. It seemed that he really wanted to connect with the people.

Just as the car drove past, I wondered how I was able to see such a prominent leader, literally at arm's length, and in full public glare, without any security checks. His security detail seemed almost non-existent that evening. The crowds began to disperse but the thought of such poor security for him lingered in my mind.

I walked back home.

At 10.15 that night, the programme on the television was interrupted by a newsflash that shook me to my core.

Rajiv Gandhi was assassinated at Sriperumbudur, on the outskirts of Chennai, where he was to address an election rally.

The telephone lines were abuzz with speculation and gossip.

Little did I know then that thirteen years later I would be deputed by Gurudev to serve in Sri Lanka when the fourth phase of the war between the LTTE and the Sri Lankan government was on the cusp of resumption.

I now realized that my Lankan story had begun long before I was introduced to the Art of Living movement.

The seed. The sapling. The tree.

~

The flight landed in Colombo and my friendly co-passenger regretted what had happened to me during my last visit to his country. 'Our country has changed now. Come home sometime. I will treat you to a nice Sinhalese lunch,' he said, handing me his business card.

Just two weeks earlier, Gurudev had asked me to accompany him on a visit to Delhi for two days. Perhaps it was meant to be a break from my routine work as the administrator of the Art of Living international ashram in Bangalore, popularly called Bangalore Ashram.

Gurudev and I were the last passengers to board the bus that was to take us to the aircraft parked at a distance on the Bangalore airport tarmac.

Two gentlemen were seated on either side of Gurudev while I stood with a black bag hanging on my shoulder. Gurudev asked me to sit, but I told him that I was comfortable standing.

The big, long bus with just the four of us took a sudden, sharp turn. I was about to fall when I quickly caught hold of the grab rail.

'He is really strong . . . isn't he?' remarked Gurudev, pointing at me and looking at the two men who smiled back.

I didn't realize that his comment was possibly a hint of what was to come—putting my real strength to the test. I learnt a lot during the Delhi trip and got back to Bangalore rejuvenated.

A week later, Gurudev left for Germany.

On the night of 30 December, he called me and said, 'Go to Sri Lanka now and do some relief work. The tsunami has caused extensive damage . . . be a bridge.'

The last three words were very intriguing. But they stayed with me.

~

My first day in Colombo took me through the city to reach Gauri aunty's house, my host and hope for several weeks. The suburbs resembled an Indian city, except for the low density of population and pollution-free air. The pristine seaside was calling to me.

I settled in the predominantly Tamil locality of Wellawatte in the heart of the city. It looked like mini-Chennai.

Aunty went to great lengths to offer food to the local volunteers who kept visiting her home for meetings to discuss our outreach and progress on the tsunami relief work.

The very day I landed, I began visiting the different areas of Moratuwa, teaching breathing techniques, hoping to relieve the survivors of their trauma.

Many participants in tsunami relief camps were still finding it really difficult to close their eyes, even while sleeping, since the scene of their families being washed away still haunted them. It was a common theme across camps.

Used to their comfortable sea-facing homes, they hadn't realized they would be living in crowded school classrooms that served as makeshift relief camps.

Suraj, Sriram, Satchi and Sumi sat down with me one evening to take a short break from the hectic activity in the camp. They had already been through enough mental trauma and agony.

I was just getting to know the Art of Living volunteers in Sri Lanka.

Sumi offered me a cup of tea, which I politely refused as I don't savour tea nor its distant cousin, coffee.

She encouraged me to have a cup of tea saying Sri Lanka produced the best tea in the world and that the Indian origin tea-leaf pickers, living in the central region of Nuwara Eliya, had worked hard to get the leaves to us.

'Warm water should do for now,' I replied.

Sipping his tea, Satchi said, 'Looks like Sri Lanka karma has started for you now.'

I laughed it off. It's an old story.

In August 1983, when I was still in school, eight new students joined our class almost three months after the academic year had commenced. It was unusual.

David and Murugan from Jaffna sat next to me in class just after we returned from a two-week break—jokingly referred to as 'Sri Lanka holidays' by us. I was happy to hear that the mathematics test had been cancelled. Numbers left me numb!

As kids, we did not realize the gravity of the situation.

This was a time when educational institutions would be closed indefinitely due to massive student protests across

Tamil Nadu, condemning the 31 July 1983 riots in Sri Lanka, commonly known as Black July, in which hundreds of Tamils were massacred, looted or burnt to death. Though anti-Tamil riots were not new to Sri Lanka, Black July was a lethal pogrom. The Tamil Nadu government had directed all schools to take in a certain number of students from among the hundreds who were migrating from Sri Lanka during that tumultuous period.

Like David, thousands of Sri Lankan Tamils were forced to flee on boats to Rameswaram, which lies on the southernmost tip of India, to take refuge. Later on, many managed to travel further as refugees to Western countries, including Canada.

'So, you already have a Lankan connection,' said Suraj, poking fun at me.

'Yes, I was a fan of Prabhakaran for his courage and fight for justice until he started the suicide-bombing tactics, killing civilians. I didn't agree with that,' I replied pointedly.

Just then, I received a call from Swamiji, saying, 'Gurudev and I will be reaching Colombo on the 3rd [January 2005]. Plan a programme and send me the details. We will be there for two days only.'

Our volunteers got together to mount a massive public programme, 'Blessings for Sri Lanka', at Colombo's largest auditorium. Hundreds gathered, including Buddhist monks and clergy from all religions, for the programme.

Gurudev led a meditation session that saw a Buddhist monk share that he had never touched stillness like this before.

Everyone needed divine intervention at that hour when the tsunami had struck the island nation a few days earlier.

Gurudev drove directly to the residence of Mahinda Rajapaksa, the prime minister, on the invitation extended by his wife, Shiranthi Rajapaksa.

After Gurudev and Swamiji had landed from India the previous evening, we waited in the special lounge for their luggage.

Ms Rajapaksa was waiting for her guest in the adjoining suite when she apparently saw Gurudev and seemed curious to know who he was.

She sent across her aide to enquire about him. I told her aide that he was Gurudev Sri Sri Ravi Shankar, a spiritual leader and humanitarian from India, visiting Sri Lanka for the first time.

Meanwhile, Gurudev and Swamiji's baggage arrived and Gurudev got up to leave. Seeing this, Ms Rajapaksa quickly walked to the lobby to meet and greet him.

As I introduced her to him, she said, 'Ayubowan. Please do visit our home at Temple Trees. We will be honoured to receive you.'

Gurudev accepted her invitation.

For several decades, Temple Trees, the official residence of the prime minister of Sri Lanka, has seen visits by many dignitaries and distinguished guests from around the world.

All morning and afternoon on 4 January, Gurudev visited several tsunami relief camps in Moratuwa, a suburb in Colombo, comforting and consoling people, distributing clothes and dry-ration kits that were shipped from India and other countries by the Art of Living.

It was about 9 p.m. when he met the prime minister, who told him at the outset, 'I have heard a lot about your social work around the world. I am happy to receive you here.'

They then had a one-on-one meeting without any aides or assistants.

We gathered later that the prime minister had expressed his keen interest to learn the sudarshan kriya breathing technique and meditation to handle the stress of those tough times.

He was not only working round the clock, but his political work must have been extremely hectic, with popular speculation that he was going to be the president in eleven months.

Swamiji was then introduced to the prime minister as the lead trainer who would share his expertise on meditation with him.

We returned to our Colombo guest house when Gurudev told Swamiji, 'I will leave tomorrow [5 January 2005] but you can stay here for a few more days. You may go to Jaffna, assess the situation there and commence our service initiatives.'

Swamiji, knowing that Jaffna was 'the hotspot' in the Lankan conflict, began to process the ways and means to kick-start our work in that region.

3

Flight to Jaffna

In 1995, the Sri Lankan government regained control of the Jaffna Peninsula from the LTTE, pushing them deep into the Vanni region that largely comprises a massive jungle terrain.

Here, the LTTE declared Kilinochchi district as their capital, which also served as their headquarters for the next fourteen years.

The Jaffna Peninsula and its surrounding areas were at the heart of the Sri Lankan Tamil education, politics, economy, culture, art and tradition for centuries. Its strategic location—just 32 km across the sea from India's southern border of Rameswaram—was indeed a huge loss for the LTTE, which had controlled it tightly for several years.

~

The week after Gurudev left for India, Swamiji's wait at Ratmalana airport was rather long. There was a single flight from Colombo to Jaffna, normally packed with forty-odd people.

'We are sorry for the delay,' said the smiling air hostess. The incoming flight was delayed due to bad weather.

Swamiji finally boarded the Aero Lanka plane. First row, second seat.

Apparently, the first seat was kept reserved for various dignitaries and personalities from civil society, religion, politics and government. While Swamiji belonged to the erstwhile royal family of Kerala, this 'prince' grew into his communist ideology in his late teens.

So the flight seat really didn't bother him nor did it make him see red in any situation, for that matter. He had been practicing meditation and was teaching it for over a decade under Gurudev's tutelage since the age of twenty-two.

Using the tools and techniques of meditation to help one lead a dynamic, happier and healthier life, Gurudev's mission as a global peace educationist is to help people return to innocence.

This shaped Swamiji and helped him in his role as the international director of programmes, a role that took him to several countries, including Russia, Mongolia, China and Japan, and some European nations to lead humanitarian and self-development initiatives.

As the flight took off towards the northern skies, he settled into reading Gurudev's book, *An Intimate Note to the*

Sincere Seeker. As he sat immersed in the book, a voice rose from the side.

'I have seen your Sri Sri on television. You look almost like him,' said a stocky, six-foot-tall man who was seated next to Swamiji, glancing at the book cover.

'Vanakkam . . . I am Thiru, the general manager of this airline,' he said, handing Swamiji his business card.

Thiru asked Swamiji about the flight and other questions typically related to customer feedback. Then, he went on to tell Swamiji about his airline's vision to help Tamils connect easily and faster with Colombo. Thiru made no secret of his loyalty to the LTTE and was looking to help them in his own small way.

'And what brings you to our Tamil homeland?' asked Thiru, sipping his tea.

Swamiji replied, 'Gurudev has sent me to help the Tamils in the aftermath of the tsunami. I heard there was massive destruction and many deaths.'

'Yes, it has been traumatic,' replied Thiru.

Swamiji's first connection was right next to him. First row, first seat!

Thiru explained vividly why he felt Jaffna needed help. He said this was just the third year since a Ceasefire Agreement (CFA) was signed in 2002 between the warring LTTE and Lankan government, and how Jaffna was slowly recovering economically and the people were experiencing a certain degree of freedom. This facilitated travel and transactions between their respectively controlled areas.

At this point, the LTTE was in a relatively stronger military position. It grabbed this ceasefire opportunity to quietly strengthen and recharge itself in every possible sphere.

However, the LTTE's covert activities continued in Jaffna, with a quiet parallel administration and low-level violence, due to various loopholes in the CFA.

Swamiji had by now received an update on the current scenario, considering his knowledge of the LTTE since his school and college days.

Thiru seemed impressed with the lengthy discussions with Swamiji. As the flight landed at Palaly airport in Jaffna, he said while exiting the aircraft, 'Let's meet sometime.'

This Palaly airstrip was the once-famous runway operated by the Indian government, when Indian Peace Keeping Force (IPKF) soldiers were stationed there between 1987 and 1990, as part of an agreement with the Sri Lankan government to bring stability in the Tamil regions of north-east Sri Lanka. This period saw a lot of hostility between the Indian army and the LTTE, leading to heavy losses on both sides.

If one thought that war was strictly a 'male domain', the LTTE shattered that myth by recruiting several thousand girls and women to fight, even on the front lines.

At 4 p.m. that day, there was a knock on Swamiji's hotel door. He thought it was the hotel staff.

He was looking out of the window, observing Jaffna life: slow-paced, lacking infrastructure and dotted with visible scars from the war.

Thiru stood there with Satya, a veteran journalist. It seemed these were men of meaningful work and speedy response.

He introduced Swamiji to his friend with pro-LTTE leanings and they sat down to get the voice recorder rolling.

'I will have this interview printed in the Sunday edition, which has a massive readership,' promised Satya Ayyah, as he was fondly called by everyone.

The interview covered the whole spectrum of the Art of Living's mission, Gurudev and his tsunami relief work, that had commenced just a few weeks earlier in Colombo and the nearby areas.

'Do you want to meet LTTE members?' asked Satya Ayyah, as he sipped hot coffee just after the hour-long interview.

'I don't know anyone here other than Thiru and yourself,' exclaimed Swamiji.

As Satya and Thiru stood up to leave, Swamiji told them to clearly articulate to the people the main purpose of his visit to Jaffna—humanitarian assistance to the people.

The following morning saw Swamiji in a minivan on his way to Point Pedro to meet a top LTTE commander.

Things had moved unusually fast since the previous evening.

The garden outside the dilapidated house at Point Pedro was overflowing with wild shrubs and weeds. The house looked as if it had been uninhabited for long. Swamiji wondered where he was and what he was going to do in a place like that, when Satya assured him that Major Illamparathy was a gem of a person. A broken wooden door opened and they walked into the dimly lit room with windows shut tight and a ceiling fan creaking every few minutes.

Satya introduced Swamiji to the Major, who looked very calm yet determined in that apparently secret location. The bold and talkative journalist then poured out more than half the things that Swamiji had told him during the interview!

The Major interjected, 'Would you please allow Swamiji to speak?'

'Satya Ayyah has played the perfect journalist,' said Swamiji, making them burst into laughter.

The mood changed suddenly when the Major asked him, 'How can you help us? We need five hundred tents immediately. Almost three thousand people have lost their lives in this tsunami.'

He made no bones about his demand. He was straightforward. Just then, three tough girls in green combat fatigues, their hair neatly braided and locked behind their heads, appeared from another room and took positions near the Major's table.

This was the first time that Swamiji was seeing hardcore LTTE fighters in person. He had only seen them in the media all these years. They stood there without batting an eyelid, obedient and determined with weapons in their hands.

It seemed like the Major was proudly displaying his coveted position in his organization in the absence of a business card.

'Let me work it out,' replied Swamiji, as they concluded a chat on the possible logistics.

'I have a meeting with the top leadership soon. May I leave?' he asked, while thanking Swamiji.

He happily received the gift of Gurudev's book when a postcard-sized picture fell out of it.

'Can I keep your Gurudev's picture?' he asked Swamiji.

Satya Ayyah smiled and said, 'We are in his safe hands now. Just take it.'

Armed with the book and picture, the Major joined his palms together in a namaste gesture and rushed through the back door.

Swamiji returned to the hotel and quickly dialled the Sri Lankan prime minister's office. After a mini dial-a-thon, the prime minister's secretary finally connected the call.

Within a week, with due government permission, a huge consignment of medicines, dry rations and tents was organized by the Art of Living. It reached Jaffna by Aero Lanka's cargo.

Our first humanitarian relief operation began successfully in the Tamil regions of the island.

'You must go and teach your trauma-relief programmes and breathing techniques to people all over Jaffna,' approved Major Illamparathy. He had called Swamiji to thank him following the fulfilment of his request.

A week later, I handed over my Colombo tsunami responsibilities to a group of new volunteers and rushed to Jaffna. Our scope of work began to expand.

Satya Ayyah had organized an introductory session of our flagship programme at Vembadi Girls' High School in the heart of Jaffna town.

At the end of the session, a woman approached Swamiji and asked, 'How long do you plan to stay here in Jaffna?'

'As long as god wants us to,' quipped Swamiji with a smile.

Naatchiyaar Amma, a feisty lecturer of Hindu Studies at the famous Jaffna University, quickly got permission for us to stay at their guest house.

'If we don't support monks, who else will?' she had told her university vice chancellor while seeking permission for our stay.

She began to visit us quite often at the guest house. She would carry with her fresh fruits and vegetables from her home, which looked like an island among sprawling green fields.

'I often tell my students to experience spirituality directly through living masters while appreciating ancient theories and concepts of Hindu philosophy,' she once said during a long and interesting conversation with us.

Naatchiyaar Amma would come over and sit for hours to imbibe Gurudev's knowledge, which helped fulfil her long-cherished dream of finding a guru, an enlightened master, in him.

One Sunday, she brought a spread of delicacies. Seeing a guest as someone really special is an integral part of Tamil culture and tradition to this day.

While serving the purple-coloured tapioca dessert, maravalli kilangu payasam, she told us, 'In the university campus, they call me "Naatchiyaar Pechiyaar" [meaning "the talkative one" in Tamil]. They think I don't know!' She laughed mischievously.

We now began to receive invitations to teach meditation to students and teachers at educational institutions across Jaffna.

Jaffna University was the birthplace of the LTTE in the early 1970s, when Tamil youth came together in large numbers and protested vigorously against the education policy and other rules and regulations by the Sinhala majority that discriminated against the Tamils.

This gave birth to civil unrest and a long-drawn-out ethnic conflict between the Sinhalese Buddhist majority and the largely united, Tamil-speaking Hindus, Christians and Muslims, that resulted in a full-fledged war in 1983.

The university guest house was a very modest accommodation that bore signs of the trials and tribulations that the people of Jaffna had witnessed—cracks on the walls, poorly maintained interiors, and broken windows and doors. In our later visits to the homes of volunteers, we came to realize that every home shared a similar fate, a testament to what a war can do: break hearts and homes.

One Friday evening three months after our arrival in Jaffna town, I was leaving Nelliady Central College at Point Pedro, located at the northernmost tip of Sri Lanka, after delivering the Art of Living Yoga and Meditation Programme to a few teachers.

Five men walked up to me. One of them asked, 'Are you from India? We have been seeing you here for the last few days.' Instantly, I replied in Tamil, 'Yes . . . I came here to teach yoga.' After a few minutes of polite conversation, a tall, stout man told me pointedly, 'The LTTE did not kill Rajiv

Gandhi . . . let's be clear on this . . . It was a plot to malign our Tamil liberation movement.'

Within a few years of the 1991 incident, an Indian investigation team had concluded that the LTTE had in fact masterminded and executed the assassination.

Now, I did not wish to discuss this topic with these young men, as Gurudev had sent me to this island nation to deliver peace education.

We all agreed to meet again the following day, when I came to know that two of these men were very close to Prabhakaran. I wondered if this was our chance to open a line of communication with the LTTE leadership.

It was a wild goose chase. They never got back to me. But it happened anyway.

Seated on a rickety old bench, I was reading a newspaper. The phone rang around 11 a.m. and Swamiji called out to me saying, 'It's Gurudev's call . . . come, come.'

The headlines that April morning in 2005 broadly hinted at the possibility of renewed hostilities between the LTTE and the government. The CFA was a deterrent to both sides, yet it was on the verge of a collapse.

'How are you . . . What's happening?' Gurudev asked.

Swamiji replied, 'Good . . . we are in the Jaffna University guest house.' I was really happy to hear from Gurudev after a long time.

'How is the food there?' he asked with great concern in his voice.

Swamiji said hesitatingly, 'We eat at the one and only vegetarian restaurant here.'

Malayan Cafe, with its 1960s benches and tables, served authentic vegetarian cuisine that was highly affordable. With flies fluttering around and an indescribable room for washing hands, we would often end up skipping the next meal and manage with just fresh fruits and water.

'Oh . . . you should cook then!' Gurudev exclaimed. I heard him and my throat went dry.

He continued, 'You know, in those days on my trips abroad . . . I would cook all by myself . . . puliyogare rice, upma or something like that . . . pack it in a small tiffin box . . . and travel and teach [meditation], meet people.'

'Why don't you start cooking?' he asked us.

I almost burst out laughing.

Here I was, already an assistant, part-secretary, part-adviser and sometimes man Friday to Swamiji, all rolled into one for my international director.

And now a cooking partnership?

Swamiji and I stared at each other blankly before replying in unison, 'Yes, Gurudev . . . we will cook.'

After a small chat with Swamiji, Gurudev wished us well and concluded the call.

The newly anointed 'chefs' set out enthusiastically for the market to buy an electric rice cooker and ingredients from the grocery stores.

We braved the heat as we walked up and down the market before returning to the guest house. We unanimously agreed to commence our cooking, in all honesty, from that night onwards.

Late that afternoon, there was a massive roar on the street. I peeped out of the window to see hundreds of people protesting and violently stoning a Sri Lankan army bus.

It had accidentally knocked down and killed a Tamil schoolgirl.

A complete curfew was declared and the army was out on the streets.

This quickly took a communal colour, souring further the relations between the Sinhalese and the Tamils.

That night, I made my first attempt to cook khichdi, a typical Indian dish.

The streets were eerily silent. Not even a dog was barking. That ghastly incident in the afternoon had deeply saddened people there.

It was 9 p.m. I soaked rice and lentils in water, inaugurating our brand-new electric cooker.

The excitement of cooking gave me a new dimension that night. Rediscovering myself.

Swamiji was engrossed in reading and I didn't wish to interrupt him, till I realized it was 10 p.m.

I set the table and asked him to come for dinner. I went to the kitchen and opened the lid of the cooker. The ingredients soaking in water stared at me. I felt they were giving me a dirty look.

Swamiji walked up to me and asked curiously, 'So . . . what's cooking? I am really hungry.'

He looked inside the cooker and saw the same thing I had discovered—raw rice and uncooked lentils. I hadn't switched on the electric cooker!

It was like a nightmare on Eelam street!

We just looked at each other, scared of what lay ahead.

He walked away quietly, retiring into the silence of the night. I slept thinking that fasting would make me much stronger.

Didn't I need an excuse?

4

The Murukku of Things

After having stayed at the Jaffna University guest house for almost a month, Swamiji and I had now moved out of that memorable place.

Our new neighbours wondered who the new inhabitants were, given that we were living in a house they considered to be haunted by ghosts and evil spirits.

Sundar sprang up from his bed. It was 5 a.m. He looked up at the sky and rushed for a bath. The cold water didn't leave him with any choice.

The war had left this stand-alone bathroom without a ceiling. It was in the mini jungle-like backyard of our house in Manipay, a locality away from Jaffna town. The house was completely neglected by the owners since they had fled from this ancestral home of theirs to Colombo during the 1983 communal riots.

Due to his expertise as a trainer of our Youth Leadership Training Program (YLTP), a very popular capacity-building programme for young minds, Sundar was deputed to Sri Lanka by Gurudev, considering his excellent skill of moulding all sorts of youth—violent, unemployed, drug addicts, delinquent and hooligans, etc.,—into upright citizens.

He began his session at 6.30 a.m. with a power-packed module of yoga. He made no bones about his discipline with the students. When he taught yoga, every muscle, nerve and tissue cried.

Deepa, a short, young woman, walked up to him and said, 'Sir . . . your first session brought out the warrior in me. I loved it. I wish I had learnt it earlier to fight better.'

He smiled, fully aware that the LTTE was well-entrenched in many homes in Jaffna. After all, he was from Nagercoil, a town in south India that was just a few hundred kilometres from the Jaffna coast.

On the third day of the programme, a bomb went off a few hundred metres from the venue. The students quickly put their heads down but Sundar, not knowing what had happened, froze in his chair. Malini shouted, 'Sir . . . Just bend down . . . head down.' He had no option but to follow her instructions. It was his first experience of a bomb blast.

After a few minutes, he asked the students if the sessions needed to be postponed and the venue shifted. Pat came the reply from Deepa, 'Sir, we are all used to this . . . but the knowledge you are sharing is new and inspiring. So don't bother; let's continue.'

A participant brought delicious murukku, which is deep-fried rice flour crafted in intricate rings to form a big ring of concentric circles, for everyone that day. This 'twisted snack' is a hit with Tamils worldwide. So much so that my grandfather would often say even the dead would wake up to snack on murukku! Observing some of his students, Sundar felt compassion. The war had made the lives of many people complicated, in a certain way 'twisted' in logic and emotions, just like his favourite snack.

One of the participants asked him what Gurudev's viewpoint was about the LTTE's justification for a continued armed struggle.

'Every war has a reason and the reason justifies the war. But the fact is that, reason is limited and as reasons change, justifications fall apart. All reasons appear to be justifiable to some limited minds and for some limited time. Hence, war becomes inevitable on this planet,' explained Sundar.

His programme was to conclude that July weekend and he invited me to motivate the group with a speech. I was there at 4 p.m. on Sunday.

I urged the youth to come forward and serve in creating a much more open, prosperous and happier Jaffna. Sundar endorsed my message and invited the participants to share their programme experience.

Deepa was the first to step forward and share, 'It was seven days of amazing transformation. My outlook on the world has changed. I feel that I have evolved.'

The participants danced and sang as we concluded the session. They just didn't want to leave. Our inspired group had now chosen to become volunteers.

Deepa, Sylvia and three others came forward with great enthusiasm to volunteer on a near-daily basis.

I was expecting a few big boxes from Colombo by an Aero Lanka flight on Monday morning.

Sundar received a call at 11 a.m., 'Please come to the LTTE office today.'

I was in the garden when he came rushing, 'They want to meet us today.'

'Who? Prabhakaran?' I laughed.

'The local LTTE office in the town,' he exclaimed.

At 12 noon, Sundar was in their office.

'You have to pay tax for any goods you bring into Jaffna. LTTE tax . . . If you didn't know,' said Senthuran.

'The boxes have Gurudev's Tamil knowledge book, Tamil bhajan CDs and tapes,' said Sundar.

'So what?' snapped Senthuran.

'We are not making any profit from it at all. It's to help people here understand Gurudev's point of view on various topics . . . Spiritual, lifestyle, yoga, meditation,' replied Sundar.

Nalini, Senthuran's assistant, intervened, 'Prabhakaran is our leader; his knowledge is enough for us.'

Sundar retorted, 'The world has opened up a lot. People here in the entire Jaffna region have been asking for his books and wisdom wherever I go.'

'Pay the tax and take your goods. No more discussion. Otherwise, give me a proposal to manufacture, print and produce all your stuff here so that our Tamils get employment, earn some money,' Senthuran remarked firmly.

'Our offices in Colombo and India have to give approval on this. I can't decide [on my own]. Give me some time.' Sundar got up to leave.

Deepa walked in and looked at him surprised, 'Sir . . . Sir . . . what are you doing here?'

Sundar explained his predicament.

She told Senthuran, 'He is my youth leadership programme teacher. They are good people. Please don't tax them.'

Senthuran laughed, 'I will send you to Vanni jungle for arms training. Don't talk too much.'

As Sundar stood up to leave, he gave Senthuran a book and said, 'Read this book written by Gurudev and call me back if you wish to.'

Deepa was in tears.

A week later, she and a few others came in a minivan and delivered the boxes.

'They will not impose tax on the Art of Living any more,' said Deepa. Sundar asked, 'Did Senthuran like the book?'

She said, 'He wants to join your next programme at Vembadi school.'

Deepa, along with many other boys and girls, had by now become huge fans of Sundar Sir. They converted our house into an Art of Living centre.

Deepa was a regular there, sweeping and swabbing the floors, cooking on some days, watering plants and distributing leaflets to promote the youth programme. She had gained our trust and confidence. Hundreds of youths started coming to participate in the training programme.

Sundar had to suddenly leave for India for a few weeks.

~

The 1990s were a turning point in the long-drawn-out civil war in Sri Lanka. Thousands were displaced and shifted to refugee camps for several months.

'My parents' generation saw women cook and stay at home. But I chose to break that trend . . . like many other girls,' Deepa told Sundar, who had returned from India after a month.

She brought lunch for us one Saturday afternoon in December as an expression of gratitude and sharing. There were nine delicious dishes that her mother and she had started preparing from 5 a.m. onwards

I was stuffed after eating a typical sumptuous Jaffna lunch, when Deepa urged me to have another helping.

Something that really touched us during our stay in Jaffna was that the people still shared with us their cup of tea, slice of bread and sometimes a full meal in spite of their war-scarred lives.

And now, Deepa was out to kill us with that delicious spread.

'You have served us a multi-barrel rocket menu,' Sundar poked fun at her, punning on the deadly multi-barrel rocket launcher (MBRL) that the Sri Lankan military fired towards the LTTE side.

Deepa took the joke in her stride and replied, 'That's what injured me many years ago while fighting a battle and I was transferred to another department to do administrative work.'

Puzzled, I looked at her. Though I had known her for quite a while now, I suddenly felt that I didn't know much about her.

'What kind of administrative work?' I asked.

She gave me a cold stare and walked away to return with some rice payasam. Serving me two bowls, she said, 'You really love sweets and desserts . . . don't you?'

I wondered how on earth she knew such a personal fact about my food preference.

Sundar looked at me and retorted, 'I never told her anything. She's just guessing.'

I looked at Deepa and praised her, 'Good observation!'

She said, 'Brother . . . I left the LTTE long back. I have nothing to do with them. Absolutely nothing.'

They had recruited her as an operative in the early 1990s, after her father died serving the Tamil movement for over a decade. Prabhakaran had known her father and his skills well since the 1980s.

She told us about a very heart-wrenching scene she saw one day: an aged mother from Batticaloa was crying her heart out and pleading with some LTTE operatives to set her teenaged daughter free from fighting on the front line. The old woman died of a heart attack in the scorching sun and the mid-level LTTE leaders just drove away after instructing some sidekicks to respectfully take her body back to her home town on the east coast.

This thought-provoking incident left her pondering about the practice of recruiting child soldiers. She finally decided to quit the LTTE. But she left behind in the power-packed cadres her brother, who was known as a brave soldier, while she returned to Jaffna to take care of their ageing mother.

Did she hang up her war boots then? 'Yes . . . the war boots . . . Yes,' she replied.

Sundar and I then left for a meeting convened by the government agent at the Jaffna secretariat. The officials had sought a proposed plan of activities from all non-governmental organizations in Jaffna district for the next one year.

I had left my cell phone behind in a hurry and Sundar chided me for that. I rushed back to the house.

As soon as I entered the living room, I saw Deepa holding my phone in her hand. As soon as she saw me, she dropped it, saying, 'The game on your phone is fun.'

I asked her to go home, saying that her mother must be waiting for her anxiously. 'Thanks for the lunch. Please tell your mother,' I told her.

I locked the house and quickly rushed for the meeting as Sundar and I had to return before the 7 p.m. curfew.

5

Lotus and Temple Trees

A few months later, when the tsunami exigencies had settled down, Swamiji and I called on Mahinda Rajapaksa to invite him for our silver jubilee celebrations in February 2006 in Bangalore, India.

'When I met him in January, Gurudev had told me that you would teach me breathing techniques to help me relax. Can we start the sessions tomorrow?' asked the prime minister.

'Yes. What time would suit you?' asked Swamiji.

The prime minister immediately called one of his secretaries and asked her to make an appointment for 6.30 a.m. for three days, starting the next day.

That week, the prime minister was unanimously nominated as the presidential candidate for the upcoming elections.

After learning the sudarshan kriya, he remarked, 'This is so relaxing yet energizing. Magical. How does this work? You must give this to Prabhakaran and his people too.' He laughed aloud.

Swamiji replied, 'You should ask Gurudev that.'

The Rajapaksa family boasted an impressive political lineage. Mahinda's father was a parliamentarian from the Sri Lankan coastal district of Hambantota in the deep south. Law studies, party politics and governance were all around their ancestral home, Carlton House.

Mahinda's other brothers also took a keen interest in these areas, except Gotabaya, who went on to serve in the army and became the defence secretary during Mahinda Rajapaksa's tenure as president from 2005 to 2016. Gotabaya became the president of Sri Lanka in 2019.

In September 2005, Mahinda Rajapaksa was busy campaigning. In the midst of his hectic schedule, he invited us to Temple Trees once again for a follow-up session.

He remarked during breakfast, 'I do the breathing technique even in the helicopter . . . when I go campaigning. It relaxes me instantly.'

'Time to fly high,' I remarked. He laughed, holding a glass of orange juice in his hand, and asked me to have one more sandwich.

In November, he won the elections and was declared the sixth president of the country.

When the LTTE strategically asked the Tamil population to boycott the elections, headlines across the world declared that a 'hardliner' had been elected.

This catapulted him to power, with the LTTE deliberately wanting 'a hawk' in that position after having replenished and strengthened itself during the three years of no war following the signing of the famous CFA.

A chance arose in February 2006, wherein the warring parties agreed to peace talks that were facilitated by the Norwegians. Unfortunately, this attempt failed in Geneva and the warring parties agreed to meet again that October. This initiative was closely watched by the international community and was also a cause for deep concern since the talks remained inconclusive.

Later, during one of the visits, the president asked Swamiji if he could check with Gurudev about speaking to him about some really important matters.

Then the telecon happened.

~

Gurudev's passion for peace is rooted in the wisdom that one's very own nature is peace, joy and love. I love this insight which forms the basis of Gurudev's peace education. Then why does man still go to war and get embroiled in conflict?

In early 2006, Gurudev was specially invited by the famous Maha Bodhi Society in India to help establish normality in Sri Lanka. He was uniquely placed to do so as he was a key member of the thirteen-member Committee for Peace in Sri Lanka, that was instituted by the society. The role of Buddhist organizations in both the countries—to help foster cultural relations and strengthen people-to-people contact—was highly imperative at this crucial time as signs of a renewed war were apparent.

Later that year, Swamiji stood with some Sri Lankan Tamil dignitaries on the vast balcony of the Buddha hall on the top floor of Vishalakshi Mantap auditorium at the Bangalore ashram of the Art of Living. Crafted as a bloomed lotus, this architectural marvel, skilfully engineered with elephantine pillars and 1008 petals sculpted intricately, beckons millions of people from around the world.

For several years, politicians of various hues and shades, ideologies and idiosyncrasies had doubled up as peacemakers, staying focused on political packages and solutions. The need of the hour was bipartisan mediators.

It was on this theme that we sought to engage with some Sri Lankan Tamil scholars, academicians and members of Parliament at a 'meet-and-greet' event with Gurudev at the Art of Living international headquarters in India.

'This marble floor is really cool,' said Suresh, a Tamil member of Parliament.

'Yes, much cooler than the war scene warming up back home,' quipped his colleague.

Suddenly, they spotted Gurudev arriving via the red-stone pathway below, which had beautifully manicured lawns and flower beds on either side. The view from the top made his flowing white robes look like a cloud floating swiftly towards us.

He received petition letters, flowers, garlands and greetings from the crowd lining up along the way.

Swamiji led the guests back into the hall. Many of them seemed excited to see Gurudev for the first time.

He opened the session by enquiring if their accommodations and the facilities provided to them in the ashram were comfortable.

'It's like heaven here,' said Suresh.

A scholar asked Gurudev, 'What role would you play to help bring peace in Sri Lanka?'

He smiled, saying, 'Being a bridge.'

He added, 'A portion of a bridge has to be on one bank of the river and another portion of it has to be on the other bank. A bridge cannot have its feet only on one side. It has to have its feet on both the sides.'

Smiles spread through the hall. When I got up and sat in the last row, I also saw doubt, surprise and a sense of relief writ large on some faces. I didn't want to see the same pessimism that I had seen in some sections of Tamil society.

A guest whispered to me, 'If Gurudev is Tamil, why isn't he only on our side?' I kept silent.

'An unbiased role, Gurudev?' quipped Joseph from the front row.

'Absolutely . . . as you know a mediator . . . a peacemaker has to be unbiased, neutral, just like a judge,' replied Gurudev.

Since the mid-1990s, several Tamils from around the world had been meeting with him during his visits abroad to seek his guidance to help resolve the issues of the Sri Lankan Tamils.

A calming breeze blew through the hall and some papers held by a parliamentarian in the front row flew away.

'If we don't close that one window, then things will be gone with the wind,' remarked a guest sarcastically. His comment evoked laughter from the crowd.

Some guests then began to make various suggestions and comments that ranged from the bizarre to the ridiculous, like asking for the Tamil regions of Lanka to be merged with Tamil Nadu to become a part of India.

Two guests now stood up and began to argue with each other, while we watched the freedom of expression play out in all its forms.

Gurudev heard them all and then said that the Constitutions, and territorial integrity of both India and Sri Lanka had to be respected.

There was a certain sense of fear on their faces when a dignitary alleged that Mahinda Rajapaksa, who got elected as Sri Lankan president in November 2005, was breaking and dividing the Tamils ruthlessly with money, promise of positions of power, titles and other sops.

'What do you think we should do? Our war is justified,' asked another parliamentarian.

Gurudev replied, 'A fight is rooted in righteousness and every side involved feels they are righteous. Without it, they don't have the strength to fight. Your sense of righteousness depends on your perception and your perception can be erroneous.'

He explained to them a key insight from the famous Indian epic, the Mahabharata, where Arjuna's perception of war was erroneous and made him lose his willingness to fight. Lord Krishna had to correct Arjuna's perception, after which he gained the valour to fight skilfully.

'This is the time to correct those perceptions on either side. Rebuild trust and confidence,' emphasized Gurudev.

'I believe you spoke with Anton Balasingham in the UK?' asked an eager lawmaker.

'Yes, I did speak to Anton . . . I was told that he was the peacemaker from the LTTE. He agreed to meet me but somehow that didn't happen. His health was a serious issue too,' Gurudev remarked.

Maheshwari said, 'We are sitting in "Buddha hall". The Sinhala Buddhist chauvinism is not what the Buddha had preached. What do you think is the Sri Lankan government's position towards us?'

Gurudev said, 'Willingness to talk. President [Mahinda] Rajapaksa had told me that he is willing to sit with Prabhakaran and have an open talk, one-to-one. He has urged me to make this meeting happen.'

After a light pause, Gurudev added, 'I feel now that valour and willingness must meet. Definitely.'

A few members of Parliament clapped on hearing this.

Gurudev urged the Tamil parliamentarians that both warring parties must meet in an open and informal atmosphere and talk in a free and fair manner without preconditions or political overtones at the outset.

Gurudev believed that this was the very first step towards helping break the ice.

In particular, he emphasized the role of meditation towards promoting an open mind. This was one of the secrets to his highly successful peace initiatives, when he broke the deadlock in talks between the government of Columbia in Latin America and its separatist rebels in 2017.

This in my view was a powerful and meaningful step in bringing 'soft power' to the table, that perhaps none had attempted previously.

Deep fear, mutual mistrust and suspicion had brought the situation to this point in the beautiful island nation and these feelings had percolated to almost every level of society.

He reminded them that even in the times of the Mahabharata war, after a day's heavy battle and when the sun set, it was normal for adversaries to meet, talk, play board games and dine together.

'What's the way forward that you suggest?' asked Suresh.

'Man's reason, as his knowledge is limited, often turns out to be unreasonable. Only when people become sensible, rise above hatred and have heightened consciousness can war be stopped,' said Gurudev.

'But how can we ordinary people achieve heightened consciousness?' asked a curious member of Parliament. 'Meditate,' replied Gurudev.

He continued, 'War is limited to humans. Since time immemorial, only mankind has been engaging in war. No other species engages in mass destruction. Animals have their prey and let everything just be.'

One of the guests recorded the audio of the entire proceedings on the phone. After the meeting, I asked her what she planned to do with the recording now. 'Obviously . . . I will send it to Prabhakaran,' she smiled.

Gurudev led a meditation session and then we left to have lunch at one of the world's largest kitchens at the Bangalore ashram.

During my tenure as the ashram administrator, two men had argued and fought over some disagreement. I gave one of them a patient hearing and concluded that the other was at fault.

When Gurudev returned from Germany, he called me to his kutir or residence to enquire about the incident. He then told me that when one stands at the foot of a hill, one will not know who was climbing up the hill from different directions. In times of conflict, it is imperative to take a top-angle view of the hill.

He opened his eyes wide and raised his shoulders, opening his palms to enact that view, as though looking down from the sky. Then, one knows who is climbing up from different directions.

This metaphor highlighted the fact that one needs to consider all points of view and talk to every party involved before jumping to any conclusion.

By mid-2006, Gurudev had ascertained an updated viewpoint of every stakeholder, influencer and support group in the Sri Lankan conflict.

Prabhakaran was the only missing link.

6

This Lime Had a Story

With great anticipation, I sat on the first-floor veranda of this two-storeyed house in Kohuwala, Colombo. That too on Valentine's Day in 2006, when I was scheduled to deliver the Sri Sri Yoga classes to a group of really keen students at our yoga studio.

I was not one to believe in psychics, black magic or any kind of occult practice but I didn't want to disappoint Mrs Fernando, a soft-spoken and devout Buddhist.

I grew up in a modern and progressive household, with a globe-trotting father who had opened my mind to world views, languages, cultures and traditions, while my mother took care of every aspect of my life at home. Learning French in school and having to eat with a spoon and fork at home complemented my Indianness at heart.

Mrs Fernando was seated next to me and had been insisting that I meet Maniyo. I had resisted several times but this Saturday was different.

She once told me that Maniyo is an unofficial title for people who follow the ten principles of Lord Buddha in their daily lives. Laypersons normally follow five principles. 'Okay . . . Let's meet her,' I finally agreed reluctantly, after three months. Mrs Fernando laughed. Almost devilishly.

The clouds of war were gathering over north-east Sri Lanka. A whole procession of violence played out almost every other week that year.

The LTTE had a 'new weapon' this time. I am not talking about the infamous explosive belt, but the deadly remote-controlled claymore bomb which was an improvised explosive device filled with hundreds of nails or steel balls.

As we were waiting in Maniyo's home, a young lady was leading a frail old woman towards a small room. Dressed in a white saree, she paused to look at me and flashed a benign smile. There was an amazing coolness and love emanating from her.

Mrs Fernando stood up respectfully and I followed suit. I was told that the old woman was enlightened and I had laughed on hearing this before.

Her daughter came up to us and said, 'Please come in . . . she is calling you.'

Dressed in a white kurta and pyjamas, I greeted her, 'Ayubowan.'

'White suits you,' she replied in Sinhalese. I smiled back saying that it was my favourite colour.

She said a prayer and then started blabbering gibberish in a soft voice.

Apparently, that was her style and format. Her daughter stood there, interpreting those sounds to Mrs Fernando, who in turn translated them into English for me.

The translation was: 'Go back to India for a few days . . . your master is waiting for you.' It had been almost nine months since I had visited India. I had neither seen Gurudev nor my parents in Chennai.

Maniyo took the big yellow lime that she had asked us to buy and slowly circled it around me in both clockwise and anti-clockwise directions. My eyes were closed.

She then gave the lime to her husband and asked me to go with him. On the same floor, there was a small altar with an idol of a deity. As we stood there, the man sliced the lime into two.

I was shocked. A whole lot of red liquid oozed from inside the lime. It looked like blood. Most importantly, this was the lime that I had bought!

Her husband looked at me and said, 'This is too much . . .'

We walked back to the room where Maniyo was seated. As she saw the lime she said, 'Take care of yourself . . . someone is stopping your master from bringing peace to our land.'

I wondered who and why would someone stop a peace process. Were there wheels within wheels?

I didn't want to hear nor believe this.

She patted me on the back and broke into gibberish again. Her daughter said, 'Your master is the one who can stop this bloodshed between the Tamils and the Sinhalese.'

The lime had a story to tell. I was stumped.

All along, I had noticed that Maniyo's eyesight was weak but little did I realize that she could see beyond.

She got up and walked away quietly.

I thanked her by saying, 'Bohoma stuti.' As a token of gratitude, I offered some Sri Lankan rupees on a plate full of fruits and a box of sweets.

Maniyo waved a blessing sign and walked away.

Though what had happened was difficult for me to digest, considering my ultra-urban attitude, I couldn't stop wondering who was trying to stop Gurudev.

That same evening, I was to meet with an official from the Indian embassy over tea and samosas.

~

The undeclared war was slowly gathering speed and so was the summer. The unforgiving April heat did not stop us from preparing for Gurudev's first visit to Jaffna in 2006.

The Tamils were going to receive a global spiritual leader on their soil after many years. The principal of the Jaffna Hindu College proudly said that Swami Vivekananda was the last to visit their premises on 24 January 1897 to give a speech on Vedantism.

At the special volunteers' meet two weeks prior to the event, the principal readily offered his school's playground for Gurudev to address the masses. It was a gesture of gratitude that the principal claimed he owed to his teacher, Sundar, who had helped transform several lives, including those of the students, teachers and the principal himself, with the magic of sudarshan kriya.

Sundar had presided over this meet, which saw over a hundred bubbling Tamil youth.

'I will take charge of the stage and decorations,' yelled Deepa. She asked Sundar a whole range of questions, often interrupting the meeting, on the kind of food Gurudev loved, who would wash his clothes during his stay, who would prepare and clean his room, etc. She was anticipating that she would get a good chance to serve and watch Gurudev in close proximity.

Many others began to offer their time and resources so that the programme would be a success.

The scale and magnitude of the event was unprecedented, with hundreds of schoolchildren planning to sing popular Thevaram songs that are steeped in Tamil philosophy and culture.

Twenty different teams, a total of several hundred youth, were finally formed to get things moving. Some agreed to sponsor full-page advertisements in print media, while others wanted to provide free snacks and milk to the thousands of students who were participating in the welcome choir.

An energetic group of women had drawn colourful geometric designs with powdered rice flour, traditionally called kolam, on entire stretches of roads, signifying auspiciousness.

Late one night, Sundar received a call from the LTTE. They wanted to set up their own camera at a strategic location to record the proceedings. On the actual day, they mounted not one but two cameras at vantage points.

Deepa said she wasn't surprised and that we couldn't refuse them permission to do so.

Gurudev landed in Jaffna on 7 April 2006, just before noon, from Colombo, when a few Tamil parliamentarians were waiting at the house where he was to stay. A week earlier, they had conveyed to Swamiji that a meeting with Prabhakaran could be fixed. During their meeting, Gurudev had told the parliamentarians that he had had discussions with the ambassadors of several countries, who wanted to know India's stand on the Sri Lankan Tamil issue. This was imperative towards shaping their stance, considering India's crucial role in the region. Gurudev then invited the parliamentarians to lunch, where one of the lawmakers requested him to keep the following morning free of any appointments so that he could travel to any secret location chosen by the LTTE leadership for a meeting.

I also recollect that in one of his many visits Gurudev had held extensive discussions with Robert O. Blake Jr, the then United States Ambassador to Sri Lanka.

Just after the MPs left, an anonymous caller told Sundar in a serious tone, 'Don't blame us if anything untoward happens. We have already declared a lockdown.'

'Why? What happened?' Sundar asked.

The caller shot back, 'One of the top leaders of the LTTE in the east has been killed . . . Cancel your event.'

Sundar didn't want to tell Gurudev about the call as the latter had just set foot on the Tamil soil for the first time.

The event was already making headlines. That phone call wasn't good news and the issue had to be addressed.

A little after lunch, Sundar gathered the courage to update Gurudev on the new development.

'Was it a threat call?' asked Gurudev. 'It sounded more like he wanted us to be cautious,' replied Sundar.

'Call him back and invite him to come and meet me. We can talk,' he replied.

However, the call never went through to the anonymous caller. Even after several hours.

'Let's go ahead with our programme,' Gurudev told him two hours before leaving for the venue.

Thousands turned up that evening from all the Tamil regions of Sri Lanka to see and listen to Gurudev. It was a sight to behold—this ceasefire zone was learning to celebrate collectively once again.

Schoolchildren danced and sang as Gurudev arrived to a tumultuous welcome. Fireworks burst in the sky and a roar of applause swept the grounds as he took the microphone in his hands.

He addressed the crowds, saying that his dream to visit Jaffna had finally materialized and his prayers were with those who had suffered and died in the war and the tsunami. He urged them to come together to bring peace and happiness, the singular goal of the Art of Living. A question from the audience was posed to him, 'Would you be willing to meet our leader Prabhakaran?'

He retorted, 'Yes. Why not? He also belongs to me.'

Gurudev never refuses to meet anyone. He staunchly believes that everyone has some goodness within them and it is possible for people to change.

The following morning, the island people woke up to headlines and photographs of the Jaffna event. Not wanting to miss that all-important call from the parliamentarians, even by mistake, Swamiji did not switch off his phone or keep it on silent mode all day. After all, it could prove to be a breakthrough event.

Gurudev visited the beach and took in a few sights of Jaffna—the famous library that was burnt down in 1981 by the Sinhalese, an act that destroyed ancient Tamil manuscripts and books, and the Jaffna Fort, that had seen many battles.

Swamiji received a call while leaving the famous Nallur temple, which draws huge crowds from abroad for its annual festival.

The parliamentarian told him, 'Sorry. We have no invitation from the LTTE.'

Sundar was thoroughly disappointed on hearing this, when Gurudev comforted him saying, 'Never mind. We will keep our efforts on.'

I believe this was the LTTE's first missed chance for peace. Gurudev and his entourage took the seaplane to Kandy.

7

The Silver Pendant

Gurudev flew to Kandy, a picturesque hill town where the famous temple that houses the relic of Buddha's tooth is located. This short visit saw Gurudev meet with the high priests of the Buddhist clergy who had tremendous influence over the Sinhalese-majority people and government. They appreciated his efforts to bring the Sri Lankan government and the LTTE together for meaningful peace talks.

Aboard the helicopter from Kandy to Wellawaya, Gurudev looked down at the rich, green expanse of hills and forests and remarked, 'This country is gifted with many ayurvedic herbs.'

Later, when Swamiji told me about Gurudev's remark, I was reminded of the episode from the Ramayana in which Hanuman was asked to fetch the sanjeevani booti (a legendary herb) from the Himalayas to save the life of Lakshman, Lord Ram's brother, after he falls unconscious while fighting Meghnad, Ravana's eldest son in Lanka.

We drove down beautiful stretches of thick forests and quiet one-horse towns and villages to reach Kataragama.

Centuries-old banyan trees and rocks stood there like silent witnesses, watching millions of pilgrims who came there every year.

We arrived at the famous Kataragama temple in south-east Sri Lanka, one of the abodes of Lord Murugan, also known as Lord Karthikeya, the deity of strength, valour and beauty.

I was surprised to see Deepa waiting for us there.

She told me, 'I wanted to follow Gurudev wherever he went. How could I miss this chance?'

Gurudev walked to the temple hall and was silent all along, though hundreds of people were jostling with each other just to catch a glimpse of him.

While a priest stepped forward from behind the curtain and offered him a plate full of fruits, Gurudev stood there with his eyes closed. The priest welcomed him with a garland of red roses and applied sacred ash, known as vibhuti or bhasma, on his forehead.

'I am very happy to see you here. We are fortunate to have a spiritual guru from India,' the priest said in an excited tone.

This is one temple that people from all religions visit to seek blessings, while many wilfully accept the sacred ash as a souvenir of grace.

In particular, both the Sinhalese and the Tamils, including those from India, have deep respect and faith in the deities and aura of this temple.

Many people from both the communities pray fervently for victory in the Sri Lankan war. So, who would the deity favour? This question struck my mind each time I visited this temple.

In Sinhalese, 'Hari' means 'Yes, okay', while the Tamils say 'Om' for 'yes'.

In India, especially in the central and northern parts, where one commonly says 'Hari Om', it carries a very beautiful connotation. Gurudev, in one of his most famous guided meditations, has said that the syllable 'ha' in the word 'Hari' signifies pain and misery, while 'ri' denotes 'relieving or relief'.

When the syllables 'ha' and 'ri' are pronounced together, 'Hari' comes to denote the relieving of pain and suffering while 'Om' represents peace and love.

I wondered why in a country like Sri Lanka, where these words are used so often, was peace elusive.

Perhaps nature was waiting for the Sinhalese 'Hari' and the Tamil 'Om' to unite first.

Gurudev conducted the very same meditation for all the people who had gathered there. The crowd, infused with serenity and joy, was unwilling to let go of him. But he skilfully slipped through the massive crowd and we drove away to the guest house.

The moon looked extremely close to the earth that night.

Gurudev told me, 'Set the dinner table outside in the garden. I will come and serve.' It was 8 p.m. and we were all famished after a long day.

We gorged on fabulous Sinhalese vegetarian food and ended dinner with curd laced with kithul jaggery syrup, locally called kithul peni, a typical sumptuous village dessert served in mud pots. With more than the expected number of guests, there was hardly any food left in the kitchen.

We settled in the garden just outside Gurudev's room. The stillness of the Kataragama pilgrimage town coexisted comfortably with croaking frogs, chirping crickets and other insects. Perhaps the country needed to learn more from nature's peaceful coexistence here.

Suddenly, I heard some loud sounds coming from the gate. I saw Deepa arguing with the security guard. I shouted out to him to let her in.

She was sweating as she walked in with her light travel bag. She told me that she had been busy helping wind things up at the venue.

Gurudev looked at her and asked, 'Have you had dinner?'

In what seemed to be her first conversation with him, she replied, 'No.'

He asked me to bring her some food. I hesitantly told him in a low voice that the food was finished and only his portion was left. I added, 'Give me ten minutes. I will get something cooked for her.'

Without a second thought, Gurudev asked for his food to be served on a plate and brought to him.

He gave her that plate.

I saw tears well up in her eyes. She dropped the bag and stepped forward. I directed her to the dining hall. It was such a heart-warming moment.

Gurudev then began distributing little silver pendants to everyone. The pendants were engraved with intricate geometric patterns of triangles facing upwards and downwards in varying sizes and sealed with a dot in the centre.

Deepa was the last to receive the pendant. Happily, she strung it on a thin silver chain.

Gurudev silently walked back to his room while Deepa rushed to catch the last bus to Colombo.

8

A Vision Dwarfed by Politics

As Gurudev reached Colombo, a series of meetings were arranged between him and a few dignitaries. One among them was with the Norwegian ambassador to Sri Lanka. The diplomat invited Gurudev to join him on a trip to Kilinochchi, the LTTE's de facto capital, to meet with Prabhakaran.

To me personally, this was a really good chance to negotiate for lasting peace. The diplomat suggested to Swamiji that we should seek consent from the Indian government, in line with protocol.

Swamiji spoke with a senior Indian official posted in Sri Lanka, updating her on the new development while requesting her for advice on how to proceed in the matter.

She said, 'Please hold on. I will need to check with the minister concerned.' Swamiji replied, 'Sure. We'll wait to hear from you soon.'

Within a few minutes, he received a call from a senior minister in the Indian government firmly saying, 'We can't have Gurudev meeting Prabhakaran now. It is election time in Tamil Nadu.'

Given the gravity of the situation in Sri Lanka, Swamiji was taken aback. He thought for a moment, somehow wanting to work it out, and suggested, 'You may wish to confer with the prime minister.'

The minister replied with palpable tension in his voice, 'How do I tell him . . . What to tell him?' It seemed quite obvious that the minister did not want to discuss this further.

Elections were on in full swing in Tamil Nadu, where the Sri Lankan cause was once again a major flashpoint.

Every politician, both from the ruling and opposition parties, ran a shrill campaign seeking justice, dignity and political solution that met the aspirations of their Tamil brethren in Sri Lanka.

When Swamiji shared this with me the following day, an incident flashed across my mind.

Gurudev had arrived in New Delhi from Manipur after meeting various militant groups in the North-eastern states of India.

His appointment with A.P.J. Abdul Kalam, then president, was slated for the evening. Kalam's credentials as a visionary, nuclear scientist and keen educationist made him one of the most popular presidents ever. He was a source of inspiration for the youth and children, encouraging them to cultivate and nurture a scientific temper.

'If you don't mind, I would like to join you too,' requested Indu Ma (Indu Jain), Gurudev's gracious host, philanthropist and the chairperson of India's largest media group, popularly known as The Times Group.

She was a devout seeker of spirituality.

Gurudev, along with Indu Ma, and a few others left 'Jain House' for the palatial Rashtrapati Bhavan, the Indian president's official residence.

The president received Gurudev warmly, after which they exchanged pleasantries and beautiful bouquets of red roses.

A presidential aide directed the visitors to an adjoining waiting room, so that the duo could carry on with their meeting.

'How was your Manipur visit?' asked President Kalam.

'The militants explained to me clearly why they had taken up arms and the deep injustice caused to them for many years,' replied Gurudev.

Apparently, the majority community was allowed to hold only 10 per cent of the land in their own region.

The president was very keen on knowing more.

'I told them that this could be resolved amicably without guns and violence . . . So many lives and years have been lost. I could help there . . . and they agreed,' Gurudev said.

He added, 'I am planning a visit to Sri Lanka to meet Prabhakaran.'

Kalam said, 'This is really good. Why don't we both just go together and meet him?'

He was bubbling with child-like enthusiasm. His secretary looked amused.

This innocent and authentic response from the president was perhaps not in line with his defined protocol. He had the right to an informal moment though.

'I have seen and met for many years the Sri Lankan Tamils who migrate every year to my home town,' said Kalam.

Kalam belonged to Rameswaram, which was just a few kilometres from Sri Lanka's Jaffna district.

Gurudev replied, 'The people there have struggled and suffered a lot for many years.'

'Come . . . Come . . . let us go together. Let's help bring peace there,' Kalam repeated once again. His eyes lit up with a sense of urgency.

Gurudev smiled. 'Sure,' he replied.

Then they discussed more shared interests, like music, spirituality and education.

The president called for some fresh fruits, snacks and juice for his special guest, who had now become a friend, what with his new plan of taking a trip together across the seas to meet Prabhakaran.

Then Kalam walked Gurudev out, crossing the waiting room to see him off.

Gurudev glanced across the room to check if everyone who had accompanied him was still present. Indu Ma was missing.

Gurudev wondered where she was. He thought she must have been taken on a short tour of the presidential residence. He asked his secretary to look for her.

Then Gurudev thanked the president for the wonderful meeting.

As they came to the outer lounge, the president pointed towards a distant figure and asked, 'Who is that sleeping on the sofa?'

The president's aide quickly ran to investigate. Indu Ma emerged from under her shawl, covered from head to toe, after having taken a royal nap. After all, she was in a palace.

She walked towards them gingerly.

'She feels at home wherever she goes,' Gurudev added. At this, she giggled in her trademark manner.

Everyone erupted in laughter and she requested the president, 'Can we please have a group picture?'

He happily consented to her request, following which the official photographer clicked away.

I told Swamiji that the president's gesture of offering to undertake a trip with Gurudev to meet Prabhakaran showed deep humanness in such a tall statesman. Unfortunately, politics played its part in denying Gurudev permission, dwarfing a chance for peace.

9

The Theatre of War

The doorbell rang continuously while I was busy cutting vegetables to make a classic Waldorf salad in the kitchen of the Art of Living's Colombo centre. I thought I should impress Swamiji at least this time round. He came running out of his room even as I rushed from the kitchen, only to find an envelope slipped under the door.

We looked at each other. I opened the door but didn't see anyone. I shut it instantly. I remember that eerie feeling even now.

It was the middle of 2006. Threats, bombs and violence were rearing their head once again.

I picked up the envelope boldly. A small handwritten note inside instructed us to meet at a secret location. It was from a very good friend of ours. He was getting in touch with us after a long time but wishing to meet through a secret note seemed really strange.

That rainy June, we drove to the location given in the note. Here we were with our Tamil parliamentarian friend, who didn't greet us with his usual bubbling enthusiasm. Not even a formal smile.

He gestured us to sit. He clearly looked stressed and knew very well that we were experts on that subject. I wondered if he wanted to seek help on that front.

He suddenly burst into tears saying, 'I was insulted by the LTTE, which I didn't expect at all.'

~

I was shocked to hear this because when we first met him a year ago, he was fully aligned with Prabhakaran and was more than willing to help us meet him.

The Tamil parliamentarian was one of the first persons who went all out to support our Art of Living work in Jaffna.

In 2005, he even invited Swamiji and me to stay in his modest house at Chavakachcheri, with people, hens, dogs and everyone else walking in and out. As a politician, he was open-minded. He welcomed the people in that region and was available to them almost 24/7. He told us that welfare service to people was his only motto. We stayed with him for three days, during which he took us around to introduce us to all and sundry.

A women's welfare meeting, poultry farmers' convention, war widows' assembly, unemployed youths' gathering or any other meet under the Jaffna sun, he happily introduced us at every opportunity, describing us as the 'breathing technology people'!

One night, after a sumptuous dinner, he made a stunning offer, 'Would you like to see a secret LTTE training and attack film?'

I was thrilled to bits because I had admired the valour of Prabhakaran in my school days in Chennai but the admiration had petered out after Rajiv Gandhi's assassination and the LTTE's involvement.

Our host switched off the lights and ensured that his Sinhalese security bodyguard was asleep before he went on to show the film.

'You must be really tired. Go to bed now,' he yelled out at him. Then, our host turned to us and said even though that man was Sinhalese, he bore him no ill-will and guarded him 24/7 like a brother. The Tamil parliamentarian proudly said that he always treated his guard like family.

Some Tamil parliamentarians had alleged that the Sinhalese security guards provided by the Sri Lankan government also doubled up as spies but our friend refuted the allegation.

Then, he played the secret video on his television.

We saw visuals of youth being trained meticulously. The video started with a few horrific stories of atrocities on Tamils that would make anyone's hair stand on end. This was meant to strengthen their minds to go through any eventuality, including sudden death for the Tamil cause.

Sessions on making bombs and the art of preparing detonators were all well exhibited. The Tamil parliamentarian told us that English films like *Rambo*, *Commando*, *Predator* and *James Bond* were scrutinized closely every week by select LTTE cadres to learn and plan ways to carry out their bombing missions.

We saw the entire training module and the celebration that followed. After their training, the cadres were taken on a long sightseeing tour in a bus across Jaffna. The bus halted at landmarks like temples and churches, and restaurants, where they were fed to their hearts' content. In the bus, they sang and danced to nationalistic Tamil songs, swearing to wipe out their enemies.

Were they belting out musical hits before the explosive belts?

For a moment, I wondered if our friend was 'brainwashing' us. My sleep evaporated.

I didn't want to go to bed watching these scenes of violence, but at the same time we had not walked into this 'theatre of war' without knowing exactly what the situation was like.

Midway through the film, I thought of the commitment and ingenuity these people possessed to achieve their goals.

You are ultimately consumed by what you play with in life; freedom of any kind simply can't come with firepower.

We do agree that the Tamil movement started when their beds were burning and lands churning with Sinhalese oppression but was 'the end' and 'the means to that end' going to be the same?

We reached the climax of the film, in which the last stop of the trainees was a grand and private dinner with their proud and smiling hero, Prabhakaran. After that was a photo op and handshakes, which were a declaration of their 'graduation' as the Black Tigers.

This deadly suicide squad was launched in the late 1980s. Over two hundred youth supposedly 'sacrificed' their lives, killing dozens of people, including politicians, celebrities and civilians.

When Prabhakaran was once asked in a press conference about the LTTE's use of suicide bombers, he had replied that times had changed and they had to adopt new strategies. Our friendly parliamentarian-turned-commentator told us about this event quite proudly. He served us hot milk with a pinch of turmeric powder as we three bachelors—Swamiji and I, the permanent monks, and he, enjoying 'temporary bachelorhood' with his wife and kids staying in Colombo most of the year—finished watching the film.

His excitement refused to wane and he quickly rushed to play the next video, which he told us was short and thrilling. We couldn't say no because we wanted to know our 'new subject' really well, especially when dealing with the LTTE and its operations.

I was almost at the edge of my seat as I watched an LTTE group ambush a Sri Lankan military checkpost in a brilliant move, complete with skill and perseverance. The video was almost like a carbon copy of a war movie, shot in a documentary style. The LTTE apparently had a huge video library comprising movies on violence, war, murder and ransom. In their entire history, it is said that they gathered thousands of weapons from their enemy just by carrying out similar covert ambush operations. No wonder they were considered the most ruthless guerrilla organization in the world.

We were 'educated' that every ambush they carried out was videotaped to learn and draft new strategies. This was one of their hallmarks.

Even in the case of Rajiv Gandhi's assassination, the LTTE had hired an Indian photographer to take pictures of the entire assassination sequence. It is believed that even the lensman was unaware of their plan.

This is how the LTTE got exposed. After the lensman died, his camera was found by the investigators. The camera provided clear evidence of the assassins waiting to kill Rajiv Gandhi. Otherwise, there would have been absolutely no proof of the sinister plot and its actors.

After the nearly two-hour video marathon, we had a free and frank discussion on our vision and mission with the Tamil parliamentarian. Somehow, he was convinced that if men of peace were willing to sit and watch a secret video of his organization, irrespective of its nature, it meant that we were deeply interested and open to contributing to its goals.

He was more than impressed with our pure intentions and was now veering towards the need for the LTTE to shift to non-violent means to achieve its objectives.

'Let me try to help Gurudev meet Prabhakaran,' he promised us at midnight. We left for Colombo the following day.

~

During the secret meeting several months later in Colombo's suburb, I was puzzled by what had changed this articulate young parliamentarian's mind.

This attorney-at-law and human rights activist went on to share with us how the LTTE seemed to have completely lost track of the Tamil cause and the pure intent with which it had started.

He narrated an incident. He had secretly gone to meet his boss in early 2006.

At the meeting, Prabhakaran asked the parliamentarian to share his views on 'a peace posturing' proposal to buy more time with the Sri Lankan government.

On hearing his frank and forthright views, the parliamentarian alleged that they slapped him hard while a few others tore his shirt and threw him out. Everyone else just watched silently.

The parliamentarian told us that he had to buy a new shirt on his return home to keep the incident from his wife. He added that he had never shared this episode with anyone, not even his fellow parliamentarians.

We didn't expect him to make such stunning disclosures.

'What is a leader who cannot listen to his own people? Will a Tamil Eelam be totally dictatorial . . . when our Tamil culture, society is pluralistic . . . where will we all go under Prabhakaran's Eelam then?' ranted our sweating friend, when Swamiji offered him some tissues and consoled him.

The world had heard of various aspects of Prabhakaran for over two decades, but now a Tamil lawmaker and a democratically elected representative of the Tamils, who also owed allegiance to the LTTE, was revealing his deep and private views openly.

He bared his soul with tears but he also felt that he had the constitutional responsibility of representing his people, the beleaguered Tamils who elected him.

We were stunned into silence, with neither Swamiji nor I interrupting him as he gave us another rare and updated perspective of the man that Gurudev was likely to meet.

The lawmaker apparently proffered a practical viewpoint on the political aspect of the Tamil issues and suggested that the LTTE quickly go in for a solution within the framework of a united, undivided and indivisible Sri Lanka. This enraged Prabhakaran, who told him that he didn't want any of the Tamil MPs to dilute the Tamil cause and that the Tamil Eelam, an independent nation, was clearly the only non-negotiable goal.

The lawmaker asked us to convey to Gurudev all that he had disclosed and left on a hopeful note that he would help foster an acceptable solution for the Tamils.

Swamiji and I had by now already intensified our efforts to reach out to people of all sections of Tamil society.

Several people who knew or worked with the LTTE leader had disclosed to us that behind the shy and quiet demeanour was a strict disciplinarian. He loved cooking and was fond of children but nothing like his passion for Tamil nationalism.

Given these insights, our groundwork for Gurudev's potential meeting with Prabhakaran began in full swing.

~

Colombo city was tense and on tenterhooks from July to September 2006. Whenever I stepped out, I wasn't sure if I would return. A similar feeling had gripped many other parts of the nation.

At a time when the weather is normally at its best and global tourists cherry-pick this country for a perfect island holiday, people were talking of violence and death.

Parents were scared to send their children to school as there were rumours that the LTTE was specifically targeting Sinhala-language schools. Army personnel guarded educational institutions with stringent security checks.

This was in retaliation for the Sri Lankan government bombing the Sencholai children's orphanage in Kilinochchi, allegedly a hub of child soldiers, in an early morning air raid in August.

Swamiji and I were at Temple Trees when the familiar security personnel, whom we would see often on our visits there, now frisked us. Mahinda Rajapaksa, the president, continued to work out of Temple Trees, where he had lived earlier as prime minister.

One of the security personnel said, 'We know you all very well . . . the meditation people, pious monks. But the country is seeing a tough security risk now.' Priyantha and Jagath were only doing their duty.

At 6.45 a.m., President Rajapaksa walked into the sprawling living room. He looked disturbed following a phone call.

He looked at us and said, 'The LTTE is wreaking havoc at Mavil Aaru. They are blocking a major waterway and denying water to our farmers.'

They were retaliating for lack of water supply by the Lankan government to the LTTE-controlled areas for a long time.

President Rajapaksa was livid that in spite of negotiating with the LTTE for over a week on the modalities to review and regulate the water supply to benefit all the farmers in that region, they kept increasing their list of demands only to put more pressure on the four-year-old Norwegian-brokered CFA.

A few days earlier, I had come across headlines stating that almost 15,000 Sinhalese families in Mavil Aaru, located in the Tamil-majority Trincomalee province, were denied water for their crops spread across 30,000 acres.

After we heard him out, Swamiji told President Rajapaksa, 'Let's begin our breathing-technique practice. It will calm you.'

President Rajapaksa flashed his trademark smile and we walked up to the sprawling room where we would meet often.

'That was a really energizing sudarshan kriya today,' he said as he opened his eyes, looking totally relaxed.

'It's been a long time since I spoke with Gurudev,' the president remarked, as he led us to breakfast.

I was thirsty and reached out for the coconut water when he asked me where I was staying. I briefed him on our new Art of Living children's home in Wellawaya, built for kids orphaned by the tsunami.

Swamiji decided to call Gurudev. He handed the phone to the president, who walked into the adjoining room.

Fifteen minutes later, he returned smiling. It was obvious that he had discussed the Mavil Aaru reservoir blockade or maybe more.

During our earlier conversation, the president had expressed his pain over the Black Tigers' assassination attempt on Sarath Fonseka, the Sri Lanka army commander who escaped with serious injuries just a few months ago. However, the LTTE was successful in killing Parami Kulatunga, a lieutenant general and the third highest-ranking officer at the time of his assassination.

These three events emboldened the Sri Lankan government to turn the heat on the LTTE, with aerial bombings on many of their nodal centres in the north and east to get them to withdraw from the Mavil Aaru dam region.

Thus, the seeds of the fourth phase of the Tamil Eelam war were sown, watered by this dam episode.

10

Liberation and a Helicopter

Ensconced in a sofa, I waited at the reception of the Taj Samudra Hotel. I missed the view of Colombo beach and decided to go to the first floor to gaze at the waves.

My phone rang and a woman said, 'I am here at the restaurant.' I walked there and saw my host for the first time.

She had called me two days earlier to discuss 'cooperating and collaborating' on a yoga project. She had mentioned the names of a few friends I had known, so I didn't bother to do a background check.

'Lunch is on me. Be my guest,' were her last words to me before I hung up the phone.

She enquired about Gurudev and the Art of Living's work in Sri Lanka. As I spoke, she wanted to know more about Gurudev's efforts in resolving the conflict. At the beginning, I was under the impression that she was trying to break the ice.

As time went by, I tried bringing up her idea of the yoga project she had planned to present to me. But she kept shifting back to our chat on Gurudev's peace process.

I had already finished with the elaborate meal, when she whispered, 'I am a slow eater. I take my own sweet time.'

Having decided that enough was enough, I asked her for one last time about the yoga project. She shot back, 'We can't pay you.'

I replied, 'I don't understand what you're saying . . . Ma'am.'

'We can entertain you . . . lunches and dinners from time to time.' I was baffled.

'Let's cooperate. Then things can become really easy for you,' she said firmly. She started revealing my educational details, my hobbies and more.

Just then, I realized that she was from an intelligence agency and was looking to hire me.

'I am not looking for a job, ma'am, nor can I cooperate on your terms. I am with my spiritual master for liberation and not to get entangled in such things,' I replied politely.

'All the work that we do in the Art of Living is transparent . . . the government of Sri Lanka, the LTTE, India . . . are all fully aware of our work,' I replied with a dollop of chocolate ice-cream melting in my mouth.

'Don't misunderstand me,' she replied in a worried tone.

'I haven't but I hope you've understood me correctly by now . . .' Though I was a little disappointed that this wasn't about the yoga project, I asked her one more time with a smile, 'So, when would you like to join the yoga classes?'

'Give me more time,' she said, skipping her dessert order.

'I have another meeting. Thanks very much for the lunch,' were my parting words to her. She refused to allow me to pay the bill.

Just as I left the hotel, Chandrasekhar, a friend of a friend, called to confirm our meeting. In twenty minutes, I reached his apartment at Wellawatte, a largely Tamil locality in the heart of Colombo.

'What do you want to share with me?' I asked him.

'Do you know I was with the LTTE in the early 1980s?' he asked me, as though I had done lots of homework on him.

'I am not a spy,' I told him jokingly, remembering my lunch meeting. He laughed saying, 'Where there's a war, there will be spies.'

He went on to tell me that he had joined the LTTE because of the draconian 'Sinhala-only' law legislated in the 1960s. It was the first racial instrument used against the Tamils.

In the late 1970s, he was discriminated against while trying to secure admission to a university on the basis of a lopsided 'standardization policy' that refused to consider the socio-economic standing of the Tamils in those days.

This policy reduced the chances of Tamil students securing admission in the best of colleges or universities.

Chandrasekhar then joined the LTTE and remained very closely associated with them till 2002, when he realized that the Tamil cause had suddenly given rise to many conflict entrepreneurs outside the movement.

Chandrasekhar recounted, 'Our ships were transporting every single thing under the sun, legal and otherwise.'

I asked him, 'But why are you sharing this with me?'

He said, 'I heard your Gurudev wants to meet Prabhakaran and bring peace . . . You should consider giving some funds to the LTTE to support the livelihood of the fighters. I can be the go-between guy.' His sheepish smile said it all.

'We are not into all this, sir,' I reassured him.

He began to share how diesel barrels from Kerala, foreign currency, and arms and ammunition shipped from Thailand were transported in small fishing boats, only for the LTTE to pick them up from the deep seas.

That's when they had already begun to take control of the seas through their Sea Tigers' wing.

Though I was annoyed at the outset, I decided to engage with him a little more. My one-hour chat with Chandrasekhar gave me a totally different perspective of LTTE operations.

'And how would you describe Prabhakaran as a personality?' I asked him a parting question.

'A brilliant military strategist . . . but a bad politician,' he said, laughing his heart out.

As his beautiful old wall clock chimed five times, I decided it was time for me to leave.

I thanked him and walked towards the door when I clearly reminded him that all my dealings would be above board and transparent.

~

After dinner that night, I walked on the terrace to take in some breeze, when I recollected a conflict-resolution meeting in 2003. It so happened that I was there in Gurudev's meeting room at the Bangalore ashram, not realizing that I would be part of a future conflict-resolution initiative in another country.

A Ramayana trail for me! From Ayodhya to Lanka.

A delegation had come visiting Gurudev to discuss the famous and complicated Ram janmabhoomi-Babri Masjid title conflict that had been going on for centuries. The Hindu community claimed that the Ram janmabhoomi in Ayodhya was the birthplace of Lord Ram that was ruthlessly demolished by Mughal king Babur to build a mosque.

Archaeological evidence proved this claim but the Muslim community claimed that the land belonged to them as the mosque had existed for several years. This case limped on for many decades in Indian courts. This was not just an issue of land. The faith and sentiments of over a billion people were at stake.

That night I recollected how Gurudev made unique contributions to the conflict-resolution table.

I heard him inspire the Muslim delegation to take the key step of settling the matter out of court and gifting the land to the Hindus as a gesture of goodwill in the interest of long-term communal harmony between the Hindus and Muslims.

Later in 2019, he proffered the same solution he had suggested in 2003, when he was nominated as a member of the mediation committee by India's highest court of law to help bring a lasting solution to the conflict.

Gurudev's sustained efforts at coming up with a solution and generating a powerful gesture of acceptance among all stakeholders to the conflict were massive turning points towards resolving the dispute.

This to me was a key learning from Gurudev on 'soft power' and conflict resolution. I believed that he could help with the Sri Lankan Tamil issues as well.

A billion hearts and minds were liberated with the resolution of that six-hundred-year-old imbroglio.

That's the role of a guru: to set you free.

~

A few weeks later, we hurriedly asked one of President Rajapaksa's aides for an appointment. 'He's leaving for abroad today. It's really difficult to meet him,' he muttered hurriedly.

'This is important for Sri Lanka's future,' replied Swamiji.

In an hour, we were at Temple Trees once again. There was a peculiar frenzy in the air, with all the senior ministers and a whole gamut of politicians milling around.

The president was at the white pillared portico, ready to board his bulletproof vehicle, when he suddenly spotted us.

One of his aides came rushing towards us. 'His Excellency wants to talk,' he whispered.

The president turned around and walked back into the lounge telling us, 'Tell me . . . Tell me . . . I need to leave soon.'

'It's really confidential,' Swamiji replied.

He quickly walked us up to a little office room and asked, 'What is it?'

'Prabhakaran is willing to meet Gurudev in Kilinochchi. We need your help,' Swamiji told him.

'That's breaking news. I support this fully. Tell Gurudev that I am willing to have an open, free and frank talk with Prabhakaran,' he said rushing out towards his car, when a short, army-sculpted man stopped him to give him some important update.

The president quickly called out for Basil Rajapaksa, his brother and senior adviser, and instructed him, 'Give them the helicopter. Gurudev is going to meet Prabhakaran. Give them whatever help they need.'

The president got into the car and whizzed away, while Basil gave me the telephone number of an official in the Ministry of Defence.

'They will arrange everything. I will keep Gotabaya updated,' he said, referring to his younger brother, who was then serving as the defence secretary.

Swamiji's phone rang while we were leaving Temple Trees, having satisfied ourselves with a major step that was going to help herald peace in Sri Lanka.

He told the caller jokingly, 'The temple has approved Gurudev's visit to Kilinochchi wholeheartedly. Now it's your job to get the trees in the Kilinochchi jungle to open up to the sky.'

After the call, Swamiji told me, 'It's Anandam from Canada. He has the LTTE's approval for the meeting. He has worked really hard to get this through.'

Anandam was one of the first enthusiastic and young Sri Lankan Tamil migrants who had met Gurudev in a temple in Canada to urge him to help find a lasting solution to the Tamil ethnic issue.

Anandam had apparently left Sri Lanka as a young man after the 1983 anti-Tamil riots and entered Canada as a refugee. For a very long time, it seems that he had wanted to do something really meaningful for his Tamil motherland.

As we were crossing the Galle Face beach on the western coast of Colombo, Swamiji looked out of the window of our car and said, 'Rudrakumaran, who is an attorney-at-law and LTTE's representative in North America, met Gurudev in the US.' I was quite surprised that I hadn't heard of him earlier.

He met Gurudev at the residence of an erudite professional in New York, during Gurudev's two-day stay that comprised programmes of yoga and meditation for Manhattan professionals. Rudrakumaran said that they were peaceful people and their community had suffered a lot. Now, they wanted their freedom. He sought Gurudev's help to get the US and the European Union (EU) to accept the plight of the Tamils and help remove the LTTE's terrorist tag.

Gurudev said it was possible if the LTTE leader proved himself first by walking the path of non-violence and stopped executing his own people. Gurudev also added that he had to come forward openly and declare his peaceful intentions.

Rudra ostensibly replied that they didn't want to go for peace as it would make them look like they had failed and had been rendered weak. On the contrary, the Sri Lankan government should come forward to declare its steps towards peace in a transparent manner, he added. Claiming that Norway was already with them, he requested Gurudev to connect them with more EU nations for financial assistance.

Gurudev impressed upon him that one cannot win a war with just money and ammunition, and that communication was important.

We reached home and began planning the details of the upcoming high-flying visit.

11

700 Metres

I stayed back in Colombo to coordinate with the government for anything that Gurudev's delegation might need during the visit to Kilinochchi.

Gurudev and Anandam had travelled from Canada, while Harish joined them in Bangalore. They arrived in Colombo on 20 September, just a day before he was to undertake that historic trip.

The sky was perfect that evening but thick, dark clouds of fear and tension had descended on the ground, thanks to the cycle of unabated violence between the warring tigers and lions.

That evening, we sat with Gurudev in the living room of our gracious host, Beena, in Colombo. Little scented candles were lit along the corridors of her pretty home and a handful of rose petals lay on the floor between every candle. That was her elegant and aesthetic way of welcoming us. It was a simple yet beautiful gesture.

Gurudev asked for the other lights to be switched off. The candlelight illuminated our faces.

Beena served us a soothing and special tea from Vietnam. The tea had a light aroma of jasmine and a soothing taste. I began telling Gurudev that an army official from the Ministry of Defence had argued bitterly with me on the dangerous timing of Gurudev's visit—when there was almost an undeclared war raging in the country.

All of the ministry's helicopters were on active duty during this period. This necessitated some realignments in their plans to offer us a high-end helicopter, which seemed impossible at that time. This stressed the officer even more.

I understood his plight but this flight was for a much bigger cause and the offer had come from the president himself.

The officer had thundered at me a few days earlier, 'Why is your spiritual master risking this . . . ? It is dangerous. What will you do if the LTTE shoots down the helicopter? They are ruthless fellows.'

I replied, 'My master has a knack for walking into the tiger's den. He has reformed wolves, elephants, snakes and buffaloes.'

The officer finally laughed his heart out and handed all the official papers, outlining the ministry's terms, conditions and approval. I told him about Gurudev's many initiatives towards reforming armed rebels operating in Manipur, Assam and Tripura in India. Several hundred guerrillas had laid down their weapons and surrendered to join mainstream society due to Gurudev's continuous peacemaking interventions.

I recalled him saying in one of the public programmes that he fully understood the struggles of the armed rebels, who were fighting out of jungles and not enjoying themselves there. Gurudev urged them to utilize the same energy and commitment by joining the civil society and contesting elections to serve their people in a democratic fashion. Some of them heeded this advice and even went on to win elections!

The official kept everything aside and asked me to tell him more about Gurudev's work. Our twenty-minute chat left him intrigued and in awe of Gurudev. The official even offered to drop me home.

Swamiji's phone rang. It was a journalist who wanted to interview Gurudev. The reporter was told that a presser might happen later, depending on the evolving scenario.

'Why does this beautiful country have the karma of war and violence?' Beena asked, hugging her little son. He hadn't gone to school because of a bomb scare that his principal had received via telephone two days earlier.

Gurudev explained that karma is a deep and vast mystery, and that every region and country has its own karma. In that region too, each locality will have its own karma. A house in that locality exercises its karma. Each individual in a house too has his or her own karma.

Gurudev then looked at me and asked, 'How do you live here? There's so much anxiety and negativity in the air.'

I replied, 'You deputed me here in 2004. This is my karma and karmabhoomi [workplace] now!' Everyone burst into peals of laughter.

Two years on, in 2006, Gurudev was making his third visit to Sri Lanka on International Day of Peace.

We had a light dinner and retired early that night. Before turning off the lights, I ran through my checklist for the next day.

~

It was 21 September 2006. There was silence in the morning air but a whole lot of expectations were flying around. What a mood to have on International Day of Peace! I couldn't understand the language of my own mind. The last time I had butterflies in my stomach was during my first job interview.

I sat by the window to meditate at 4 a.m. and opened my eyes an hour later on hearing Buddhist temple chants coming from afar.

Gurudev was walking in the courtyard and suddenly stopped to look at the sky. I quietly went and stood behind him when he turned and asked, 'Are we ready to leave?'

'In a few minutes,' I replied as he sat on a garden bench and lightly caressed the grass with his feet. I quickly rushed to the kitchen, picked up the lunch basket, placed it in the boot of the car and then ran up to inform him that everything was ready for the trip.

He boarded the car, followed by Swamiji, Anandam and Harish, one of our senior Art of Living teachers. I wished them well as I waved to them.

They left to take a flight from Ratmalana airport to Anuradhapura air force base, and from there by helicopter to Omanthai which bordered Kilinochchi, the LTTE's most prized capital.

As they landed in Omanthai town, the air seemed toxic with fear, anxiety and mistrust writ large on people's faces. The drums of war and bugles of fire were sharp and shrill in the collective psyche of its people.

A Sri Lankan government vehicle picked up Gurudev, Swamiji, Anandam and Harish from the helipad and passed through its famous Omanthai army checkpoint on the A9 highway.

For several decades, thousands of people had to stand in serpentine queues and go through stringent security checks while crossing from the LTTE side into government-held territory. This was to prevent LTTE operatives from infiltrating into Lankan territory.

This place was steeped in history. During the earlier phases of the twenty-six-year war, this checkpoint was apparently the place where the bodies of the cadres or soldiers were handed over to their respective sides.

The abundance of palmyra trees was a common sight in this landscape, spanning the northern parts of Sri Lanka. Both sides extensively used the tree's bark as poles and its spiked leaves stitched together as a wall to protect their respective military camps from prying eyes. This checkpoint too seemed 'palmyrized'.

The war had badly hit farming and agriculture in the border villages here, with several hectares of land rendered 'unusable' for various reasons.

Beyond this place was a place commonly referred to as 'no man's land'.

This stretch was carpeted with landmines and served as an entrance to the LTTE-controlled territory. This barren patch served as a 'buffer zone' between the Sri Lankan government and LTTE areas.

As they reached the beginning of 'no man's land', Gurudev, Swamiji, Anandam and Harish saw a small cabin run by the United Nations (UN), which acted as a neutral party and monitoring agency.

The government vehicle stopped here and the accompanying official told Gurudev that they couldn't go further as it was outside the jurisdiction of the Sri Lankan government. Therefore, Gurudev and the others had to walk from there and whatever happened beyond this point was not the responsibility of the government.

Meanwhile, a UN official stepped out and greeted Gurudev saying, 'We are yet to get permission from the LTTE side. Please wait until then.'

Swamiji told him, 'We already have the permission.'

The official replied, 'But I have no message from them . . . I coordinate all movements on this stretch here.'

Anandam frantically worked the phones to speak to a few people. He was the one who had coordinated and confirmed the appointment in consultation with the top LTTE leadership. Exasperated, he told the person on the other end of the phone, 'What's happening . . . We are waiting at the UN checkpost. They say there's no approval. How can you do this?'

Meanwhile, Gurudev engaged in a chat with the official, who pointed out to a place towards the LTTE side, just a few hundred metres ahead. 'A cow went on this road yesterday, when a landmine blew up and it died on the spot,' he added.

Gurudev continued to listen to him, while the others looked at each other and perhaps wondered how they would cross that deadly stretch of the dirt road.

The official added with great concern, 'They [the LTTE] have planted landmines all over, recruited children as soldiers. Tough life here. It's no man's land. No man's responsibility, except mine!'

The LTTE made them wait for over an hour.

All that they could see were patches of dry land with weeds on either side of the dirt road towards the LTTE checkpost. It looked like no one had grown a single grain there, with landmines replacing them. It is estimated that over the years several hundreds of landmines were planted by the LTTE in various parts of the north and the east.

Vikram was waiting in his car on the LTTE side. Three days earlier, I had sent him from Colombo to Kilinochchi with all the relevant papers. He was to drive Gurudev to the venue of the meeting with Prabhakaran.

After a while, a white flag was waved as a sign of approval for the delegation to walk across the 'no man's land'. As Gurudev began to lead the group, Harish recollected what the UN official had said about the cow. He seemed worried now.

Without batting an eyelid, Gurudev told everyone, 'Just follow my footsteps.'

The 700-metre distance took a little longer than it should have, as they walked gingerly. Every step and breath they took left them alternating between relief and caution. It was like walking a tightrope on solid ground.

One by one they walked behind Gurudev, setting their feet on the footprints he left in the soil.

Occasionally, they would see someone who looked like a teenager peeping through a small opening in the massive iron gates of the LTTE checkpost.

As beads of sweat flowed down their brows, Harish and Anandam carried the lunch basket, a box of fruits and token gifts from India.

There was an eerie silence and no sign of life, except for a few crows crowing. Suddenly, there was a loud boom. The three of them froze in fear but Gurudev continued walking. There was gunfire somewhere in the distance.

Gurudev turned and glanced at them. Placing their deep trust in him, they began to walk behind him once again.

As they reached the massive iron gates, Harish exclaimed, 'This felt like walking through eternity.'

A lanky boy in his teens, who was struggling to hold a large gun in his hands, opened the heavy gates with a lot of effort.

They quickly got into Vikram's car and drove over the dirt roads. Deep brown mud blew with gusty winds from time to time as they entered Kilinochchi town.

There were huge posters on walls glorifying LTTE martyrs and some children. Vikram told Gurudev, 'Those are pictures of the children killed in the Sencholai orphanage bombing by the Sri Lankan air force just last month.'

Some of the posters posed questions like 'Is this what the Buddha taught you?', presumably questioning the Sri Lankan government's brutal bombing of the Sencholai orphanage.

The Lankan air force justified the air raids saying that the orphanage was 'a front' for LTTE child soldiers.

There were media reports that Prabhakaran had stayed over there that night and was a frequent visitor, given his love for children. Apparently, he had left the building in the wee hours of the morning, narrowly escaping the attack that left over sixty children dead.

A few minutes later, on seeing a temple, Gurudev said 'Let's visit it.'

As everyone got down from the car, people started gathering and asking all sorts of questions like where they were from and who did they want to meet.

A group of students in white uniforms and a few adults stood gazing at Gurudev from a distance, when he called them and distributed some sweets that he had carried from India. As they received the sweets, they expected him to offer them vibhuti as a gesture of blessing, as per their centuries-old Tamil tradition.

The elderly priest from the temple handed over a bowl of ash to Gurudev, and many people began to gather to receive it with reverence.

One of the elderly recipients remarked, 'We are seeing a saint for the first time in our lives . . . that too a Tamil-speaking saint . . . We are really very fortunate to receive you in our Tamil homeland. Please come again and give us a discourse here.'

Many others agreed in chorus, 'Yes . . . Yes.'

'If we had known earlier that you were coming, we would have welcomed you in a big, grand way,' remarked the second priest at the temple.

Gurudev engaged in a conversation with everyone, enquiring about their welfare, daily lives and vision for the future, when a schoolgirl told him, 'I saw you in April at the Jaffna programme and had asked you to fulfil a wish of mine. My mother is fully cured now. She has started walking.'

Gurudev smiled and nodded.

She bowed down and touched his feet in gratitude, a gesture of respect in the Indian subcontinent.

The temple priest told Gurudev, 'I had heard about you many years ago and wanted to meet you. I have read some of your knowledge articles in newspapers. Welcome to Kilinochchi.'

He asked the priest, 'Where does Prabhakaran stay?'

The priest replied, 'No one knows. Looks like the war is starting again.'

Just then, Swamiji received a call from Gajan, an LTTE operative, 'Our man is reaching in thirty minutes. He will guide you to the place where you have the scheduled meeting with our leader. Just follow him.'

Christina walked up to Swamiji and asked, 'He [Gurudev] had visited a house in Jaffna when I saw him in April. Will he visit my house too?' Swamiji asked her to go and directly check with Gurudev.

The girl promptly walked up to him and repeated her request.

'How far is your house?' he asked her. The girl replied that it was just five minutes away. Anandam and Harish stayed back at the temple while the rest drove away, with Christina guiding the car through the lanes of Kilinochchi.

She got out of the car and pushed open a little rickety wicket gate, sending the hens and chicken scurrying away into the garden. Sensing new visitors, her dog barked continuously. Hearing the dog bark, Josephine, her mother, came out of the house and was surprised to see Gurudev.

She welcomed him into the house. It had no furniture, only two tattered mats lay on the floor. Josephine ran into one of the rooms and brought out a green plastic chair, wiping the dust off it and requesting him to take a seat.

She told him, 'I am happy you came here. When I first saw you at the Jaffna public programme and you had asked us all to make a wish, I had prayed that my partial paralysis should be fully cured. That I should be able to walk.' Tears welled up in her eyes, gratitude flowed.

Two months later, the doctors had told her that her paralysis was getting cured really fast and miraculously. She had begun to walk normally.

Josephine offered Gurudev a glass of water and asked if she could cook some snacks for him. He told her that there was a meeting scheduled and they had to leave soon. Just then, Swamiji received a call from Harish asking them to return to the temple.

Gurudev told Christina that after completing her secondary education, she could come to India on a scholarship to study at the Ayurveda college run by the Art of Living in Bangalore, inspiring her to serve people in and around Kilinochchi district.

Seeing a car at Josephine's gate, a few people gathered outside the house. Gurudev asked for the fruits to be brought from the car and Vikram placed the apples and bananas on a tray.

Many of Josephine's neighbours walked into the house. Gurudev gave each visitor a fruit as they sought blessings for their families.

Christina and Josephine ran behind the car for a few metres. After all, the wish they had chased had come true.

12

The Rendezvous

Though clouds of war were fast approaching, a near-normal life was visible with LTTE cadres milling around at certain points of Kilinochchi town.

It was interesting to note that for many years the LTTE had established its very own Tamil Eelam court of law, police stations, banks, etc., in places under its control, like any other independent nation.

They operated like 'a state' within a state!

A youth on a motorcycle led the car through what looked like the interiors of Kilinochchi. A few thatched huts interspersed with banana trees and hibiscus plants were a relief to the eyes. These plants were an intrinsic part of their day-to-day lives.

A second man on a bike joined them at a junction. He drove alongside the car and told Vikram, the driver, in a loud voice, 'You will only follow us and not stop the car anywhere. No photographs or videos. Tell this to everyone in your vehicle. Most importantly, switch off your phones.'

Vikram nodded in agreement.

Finally, they reached a house with a red-tiled roof, where three men and a woman in LTTE uniforms waited at the entrance.

Anandam started getting emotional.

He told Swamiji that he was feeling nostalgic upon returning to his homeland after almost two decades. But his nostalgia was short-lived, as his mind was now focused on making the meeting with Prabhakaran successful.

'Please come inside,' said a young man, who introduced himself as Selvam. He introduced the other cadres as Charles, Thamilini and Kumaran.

The living room had comfortable-looking brown sofas that made it seem like a place for regular meetings.

Looking at Gurudev, Selvam said, 'I have seen you on television long back . . . I feel that you can help us bring liberation.'

Swamiji and Harish settled down next to Gurudev, while Anandam stood at the door chatting with Kumaran, an LTTE operative seemingly hardened by the war.

What made these diehard cadres unique was not just their rugged personality but a certain supreme confidence that sparked their valour and a determination backed by deep faith in values and culture. If only they had used this sense of commitment and energy in a constructive manner, they could have moved mountains.

An eager Harish was expecting the LTTE supremo to arrive but could not see a swarm of armed security personnel or the buzz that one would normally expect from a personality like Prabhakaran. For a few minutes, no one seemed to have a clue of what was happening.

Charles, in green combat fatigues, decided to break the silence and said, 'All our leaders are in a meeting. We have been asked to wait.'

Swamiji looked at Anandam, who was arguing tensely with Kumaran just outside the door. Swamiji quickly took Selvam aside and told him, 'You know Gurudev has come all the way from Canada to Bangalore and then to Colombo, travelling almost non-stop. Where is your leader?'

Selvam muttered hesitantly, 'Ah . . . Eh . . . Yes, we understand . . . but . . . our leader . . . is in a meeting.'

Kumaran came in and intervened, 'Swamiji, please sit down. We are just following orders. We will let you know as soon as we get updates.'

Charles quickly stepped out of the room to make a call. Harish could hear him ask on the phone, 'Is our leader coming?'

Anandam interrupted him and said firmly, 'You gave full confirmation that he would come and meet . . .'

Charles retorted, 'Yes, we did agree that he would come for the meeting . . . So what do you want us to do now? We are also awaiting confirmation!'

Anandam's patience was wearing thin in that sultry weather. He turned to Selvam and asked, 'At least tell us where your leader is?'

They all kept silent, giving the group a cold stare. They were all apparently trained to hide their emotions and keep a straight face so that no one could figure out what was running through their elusive minds. This seemed to be an integral aspect of the LTTE's culture and character.

Even if Prabhakaran had been right there, down in a bunker under the very same meeting place, they wouldn't have disclosed it.

A restless Anandam continued, 'Why can't he come over when we have come all the way and that too with his approval? This doesn't reflect our Tamil culture.'

Thamilini, who had been a silent observer so far, said, 'The Sri Lankan government told us about the details of your helicopter flying so that our cadres don't shoot it by mistake . . . but . . .'

Kumaran walked in as she was speaking and said in a boasting voice, 'Sir, I cannot speak for our leader but one thing I can say is that we are in a stronger position now militarily. We don't have even an iota of doubt about our Tamil liberation, even though India has also betrayed us.'

Anandam stood there embarrassed, having realized that the chances of Prabhakaran coming there were bleak. Meanwhile, Swamiji and Harish were closely observing the reactions of the cadres.

At a distance, they heard some gunshots. The cadres looked at each other in complete silence and gave a blank stare. They were living up to the LTTE's culture of secrecy and remaining tight-lipped. Now all that one could hear was a dog crying at a distance. It continued whining, perhaps in deep pain.

Anandam, feeling guilty and disappointed, apologized to Gurudev for making him wait and told him that he was working on a solution.

Gurudev smiled and comforted him.

It was very evident that these operatives were low-ranking cadres sent to just keep the delegation occupied with excuses till they heard from their leader.

Though Swamiji remained calm, he couldn't hide his disappointment as they had been made to wait.

But Gurudev looked absolutely comfortable.

Meanwhile in Colombo, I received calls from various government officials enquiring about the progress in Kilinochchi. I told them that I had absolutely no clue since all the phones were switched off. One official even retorted that he was not surprised and how it was typical of LTTE norms.

An hour passed by when the cadres settled down in their chairs. The hustle and bustle melted away. Swamiji noticed a sudden change in the environment.

It seemed as though the walls around the cadres had crumbled down and something had opened up in them.

There was complete silence in the room. It was broken only by the ringtone of Charles' satellite phone. He quickly stepped out to take the call. He ambled back in after a few minutes and took Swamiji aside to ask him if Gurudev could stay on for one more day in Kilinochchi.

Swamiji replied, 'We have Navratri celebrations happening day after tomorrow at our Bangalore ashram. He can't stay on and has to leave today. Thousands of people have come from all over the world.'

However, Charles still insisted.

Meanwhile, Gurudev gave the cadres some gifts from India and handed over a pure white shawl embroidered with light gold threads.

'This is for your leader. Give it to him . . . ,' he said, 'I know you want liberation; you want to win the war . . . but it cannot be won only with weapons or force. You need *yukti* [skill].'

Gurudev got up and walked out towards the car. He had said enough without saying much. His gestures said it all.

Swamiji and Selvam were the last to leave the house. Selvam held his hand and whispered, 'I had great hope that if our leader had met Gurudev today, there could have been a certain change in his perspective. I am sorry he didn't turn up. This is a bad omen . . . looks like something bad is going to happen to us.' His eyes welled up. He quickly wiped his tears and put on a chivalrous look.

As Gurudev sat in the car, Selvam told Gurudev that his setting foot on their soil was a very big blessing for them. Once again, he asked him, 'Bless us . . . Bless us for liberation.'

The car left for Omanthai.

Anandam wept quietly, covering his face with a handkerchief. His efforts at making the meeting happen had failed. As the helicopter took off for Colombo, a cloud of dust rose from the ground below, blinding the motley group of villagers who stood gazing at the big black metal bird gleaming in the scorching sun.

Swamiji observed that the morning's perfect sky now looked torn.

A few minutes before landing, Anandam sobbed while holding Gurudev's hands. Anandam's face had shrunk in guilt, as the whole exercise was facilitated by him. He said, 'I apologize for what happened. Prabhakaran made a big mistake by not coming to meet you. This is a sign of the times to come. Unfortunate.'

Gurudev smiled and cheered him up saying, 'Your name itself is Anandam [meaning bliss or joy in Tamil] and you are sobbing. Whatever has happened, you still played your part to the best of your abilities. Now leave the rest.'

I received them at Ratmalana airport in Colombo and drove them straight to Bandaranaike International Airport for their flight back to India.

At the airport lounge, I went up to Gurudev and told him that the lunch basket was still intact. He just closed his eyes without replying.

I don't know if he even heard me. Perhaps my statement would have seemed too trivial.

Then, I walked up to Swamiji and asked him about what had happened at Kilinochchi. 'Gurudev didn't even sip a drop of water. The rest I will tell you later,' he whispered.

The airport official at the lounge told me that the flight was ready for boarding. With tears in my eyes, I hugged Gurudev.

The doors to the tarmac opened and he walked towards the aircraft that was parked nearby.

As the door shut, I felt as if a chapter had come to an end.

~

The following day, I got a call from an unknown number. It was the journalist I knew for quite a while.

'You haven't given me a good headline. Let's meet,' said the shy journalist. I went to meet him at a secret location, as per his request.

'It's not about a headline. Many heads are on the line. This decision of the LTTE leader to not meet Gurudev is very unfortunate for generations of Tamils,' I told him.

'Yes . . . I totally agree. I have an inside scoop,' he said.

'What scoop . . . ? Vanilla or chocolate,' I quipped.

Journalists around the world are pillars of society, standing tall. They have their head in the air, ear to the ground and finger on the pulse. And once in a while, a foot in the mouth too.

I knew that this journalist had deep connections with several key people in both the LTTE and the Sri Lankan government.

The journalist shot back, 'I got it from the horse's mouth.'

I retorted sarcastically, 'Thank god . . . not from the tiger's mouth.'

He said the LTTE intelligence had informed Prabhakaran of the possibility that India might quietly and indirectly help Sri Lanka by bombing him while he was on his way to meet Gurudev.

The journalist went on to explain that India could share real-time information with the Sri Lankan government on

Prabhakaran's movement with the help of Indian radars and satellite images to target his vehicle.

I told him that India would never do that. It sounded atrocious. Moreover, the Sri Lankan government had given its full approval and support for the meeting.

'This is what I was told when I spoke "to them" as to why Prabhakaran didn't go to meet Gurudev,' he said, shrugging his shoulders in a matter-of-fact way.

The journalist explained that the LTTE cadres could not even have Prabhakaran speak on the phone to Gurudev for the same reason, since the call could have been used to trace Prabhakaran's whereabouts.

I told the journalist that Gurudev and his entire delegation were in just one car and even their mobile phones had been switched off as per the LTTE's instructions. So how could anyone trace the coordinates or the place of their potential meet with Prabhakaran?

He then asked me about 'the white shawl' for Prabhakaran that Gurudev had given to the LTTE team.

The media in India and Sri Lanka had blown this aspect out of proportion, with some journalists writing their own 'black letters' about the white shawl.

Most of the pro-LTTE media said it was a sign of blessings from Gurudev to Prabhakaran and that victory was on the horizon for them.

Some even went on to suggest that this was a message to Prabhakaran to fight valiantly and without any fear.

I did receive many telephone calls asking why Gurudev had given 'a white shawl' when Prabhakaran hadn't come to meet him.

I told my journalist friend 'Gurudev signifies "one thing" . . . One thing . . . You know that too.'

He smiled and said, 'Give me a good headline next time.'

We agreed to stay in touch and I rushed back to catch my favourite Hari Om meditation.

13

The Turning Point

Two months after Gurudev's Kilinochchi visit, Prabhakaran delivered a final warning to the Lankan government during his annual Martyrs' Day speech on 27 November 2006. This event was held on his birthday where he would outline the LTTE's standpoint on various themes as well as commemorate all those people who had sacrificed their lives for the Tamil cause. On this day, relatives of the dead cadres visit their graves, marking poignant scenes across Tamil regions. A key highlight of Prabhakaran's 2006 speech was that he saw no hope in a peaceful resolution to the conflict.

He inspired his followers with these words: 'It is now crystal clear that the Sinhala leaders will never put forward a just resolution to the Tamil national question. Therefore, we are not prepared to place our trust in the impossible and walk along the same old futile path. The uncompromising stance of Sinhala chauvinism has left us with no other option but an independent state for the people of Tamil Eelam.'

It was almost an open declaration of war. Moreover, the October peace talks facilitated by the Norwegians in Geneva, after the failure of the first round of talks in February 2006, that attempted to bring the government and the LTTE to the negotiation table, had failed to take off.

A few Tamil parliamentarians had no luck either when they had knocked on the doors of the Indian government to meet the then Prime Minister Manmohan Singh to apprise him of the new stand of the Tamils. They submitted the memorandum to senior Indian officials in the foreign ministry and returned empty-handed, without any fruitful outcome.

I decided to take a trip to Jaffna to gauge the situation there before heading to India. The Tamils were preparing for all eventualities.

Each time I visited India, Gurudev's devotees and well-wishers would send letters for him. Typically, they would be letters asking for some wish to be fulfilled, words of gratitude or simply seeking his blessings.

Sylvia came to meet me. She carried with her a box of palm jaggery and some murukku that her mother had prepared for me. While handing over two hundred letters from various people in Jaffna region, she wished me a safe journey.

When I asked her where Deepa was, as she was not to be seen around, Sylvia replied that Deepa had been missing for over a month now.

I was shocked and worried.

On my arrival in India in December 2006, I requested an appointment with Gurudev. At 9 p.m., I was told to meet him after the evening satsang.

Other than meeting Gurudev, if there is one thing that anyone looks forward to while at the Bangalore ashram it is being a part of the ashram satsang.

That evening, people danced in the vast green amphitheatre like there was no tomorrow. So divine was the atmosphere that it felt like the majestic and intricately carved Garuda statue that stood there would break free to soar into the sky.

Foot-stomping music coupled with mystical lyrics praising divine qualities filled the air. The singers holding the mic sang their hearts out.

This evening of music, wisdom and meditation melted into what we popularly call 'satsang', which means in the company of truth in the Indian tradition, where hearts and minds unite and resonate in one peaceful wave and vibration. Powerful wisdom from Gurudev is the icing on the cake, making that celebration complete.

This was two months after Gurudev had returned from an apparently 'failed' step in his attempt towards helping resolve the Lankan conflict.

Slowly, as the crowd of nearly five thousand settled down, a man stood up to ask a question. A volunteer from the organizing team handed him a cordless microphone as the question-and-answer session with Gurudev was about to begin.

The man asked, 'I have been told that the human soul can often take one to two million years to find liberation.

Is it true that by doing [sudarshan] kriya and meditation every day, this liberation can be obtained even in one lifetime?'

Gurudev replied, 'Everything works with some strange karma. You must lift your eyes and look into this realm. There is a beautiful couplet that says, "This world has all the wealth, all that is needed, but one who has no karma, cannot get it". So, whether you get something or you don't, it all works with some strange karma. Recognition, money, power, relationship, health; everything depends on some law in creation. When good times come, your worst enemy starts helping you, and when bad times come, even your best friend behaves like an enemy. All these things happen due to some very strange karma.

'An intelligent person doesn't get caught up in all this. You still keep putting in the effort and keep moving on. You do whatever is needed to put in an effort, and then you leave it.

'Do you know Lord Krishna went three times to stop the Mahabharata war?

'When someone asked Lord Krishna "If you knew that the war was going to happen anyway, why did you go three times for peace negotiations? All three times your peace negotiations failed, so why did you go?" That was a very valid question.

'Lord Krishna said, "If I had not gone, then you would've asked why I didn't attempt a negotiation? The question would have come that you could have done peace negotiation, why didn't you do it?"

'You have your duty towards your karma; whatever you need to do, you do it! Suppose the peace negotiation would have succeeded, then the whole Mahabharata would have ended, and the Gita would never have come! The immortal song of the Divine [the Bhagavad Gita] would never have come into existence!

'So, Lord Krishna still attempted a negotiation, very well knowing that the Gita had to come, and the war had to happen; still Lord Krishna went for peace negotiations. This is because it is in our dharma, our nature. We should keep putting in our efforts and remain unattached to the consequences or the results. This is very subtle because the mind gets sucked into maya, 'illusion' in some form or the other.

'The mind needs to be hammered into knowledge and wanting liberation. So keep on hammering the knowledge back again and again! Suddenly, you will find it is all there, anyway.

'Whether pleasant things or unpleasant things are happening, you are a witness to it. And even your mind getting caught up in it, is a part of the happening; you are a witness to that, as well. This is how you rise above the situation! You have to practise pranayama, meditation and knowledge. The whole life itself is a practice, and when you practise with honour, then this knowledge becomes well-founded in you.'

~

The December air of Bangalore had relieved my frayed nerves but listening to Prabhakaran's clarion call to his cadres to gear up for war was disturbing. Any signs of peace seemed to have hit a dead end now. I had an evening appointment with Gurudev to brief him on the new developments in the island nation.

Swamiji and I entered Ganga Kutir, where Gurudev normally receives guests. I was surprised to see T.N. Seshan seated there. His eyes scanned and swept over us. He was one of my heroes, someone I looked up to, while I was in college. Seshan had cleansed the electoral system as the chief of the Election Commission of India from 1990–96. During his tenure, he had rattled many a politician and political parties with his model code of conduct and its strict enforcement. He soon became an icon for India's huge middle class, that was yearning for a corruption-free electoral system.

As we sat down, I heard him tell Gurudev that one of India's prime ministers had offered him the plum post of an ambassador in a foreign country but he had declined the offer politely and instantly. He told the prime minister that he already had at home an Ambassador—a famous Indian car brand in the late 1970s—and that was more than enough for his wife and him.

I couldn't hold back my laughter at his unique style and trademark humour. Seshan's wife, who was seated next to him, told Gurudev that it was her cherished dream to sing 'Narayaneeyam' in front of him. This opportunity saw her give a soulful rendition of the ancient hymn, adding flavour to the spiritual ambience.

Gurudev then introduced us to them as his emissaries to Sri Lanka, when Seshan said, 'I have fond memories of that nation when I served as the defence secretary.'

He added that he had come up with an alternate plan, beyond the Peace Accord, to resolve the Sri Lankan Tamils' situation. However, the government was reluctant to go ahead with his plan.

Fifteen years later, he had the same bubbling energy, brilliance and enthusiasm. He spoke about the Indo-Sri Lanka Peace Accord of 1987, which was primarily aimed at resolving the Tamil issues by empowering them through the thirteenth amendment to the Sri Lankan Constitution.

When the massive flow of refugees from Sri Lanka to India continued unabated due to an escalation in the conflict, J.R. Jayawardena, the then president of Sri Lanka, had requested Rajiv Gandhi to send the Indian army to play the active role of 'peacekeeping' in the north and east of Sri Lanka.

The IPKF's role was to disarm all Sri Lankan Tamil rebels. However, a few months after they set foot on Lankan soil, fierce battles broke out between the LTTE and the IPKF, with the Sri Lankan government remaining a mute spectator.

Just like Gurudev, I observed, Seshan too was a man who engaged the youth with his wisdom and sense of wit, effortlessly inspiring curious minds.

As he continued his meeting with Seshan, Gurudev asked Swamiji and me to proceed for dinner saying, 'Let us meet tomorrow morning.'

~

The following morning, Swamiji and a few others were seated in Ganga Kutir.

As I entered the kutir, he said, 'So . . . what's happening in Sri Lanka?' I told him that the fourth phase of the war was imminent and presented to him the letters that Sylvia had given me.

He suddenly got up, went to another room and returned with a little box in his hand. The box had a beautifully embroidered silk exterior with rich green motifs.

He said, 'This is the gift that I was carrying for Prabhakaran when I travelled to Kilinochchi.'

Creating an air of suspense for all of us, Gurudev opened the box. He paused for a few seconds, keeping his hands still on the half-opened box, and looked at us, perhaps to see the anticipation and eagerness on our faces.

He took out a little spear, which in the Tamil tradition and culture is popularly called *vel* (pronounced almost like whale with the 'h' silent).

Absolutely none of us were aware of this gift he was carrying with him.

'What is its significance?' asked a young lad from northern India.

Just as the holy cross is a powerful symbol of the Christian faith, the vel is one of the most revered symbols for millions of Tamil Hindus all over the world, including those in Sri Lanka, Malaysia, Singapore and South Africa.

Gurudev placed the box on the table and went on to share something mystical yet practical. We listened with rapt attention.

'The [Sri Lanka] president had conveyed to me that if Prabhakaran had taken up peace and was willing to get democratically elected, he [the president] was even ready to offer him [Prabhakaran] the position of the prime minister of Sri Lanka.'

At this, Swamiji and I glanced at each other in total surprise. We never knew about this. But maybe the time was not right earlier for Gurudev to disclose it, even to us.

Someone added, 'So is this also a play of karma that Prabhakaran didn't come to see you?'

There was total silence. I told him of the letters that some devotees from Sri Lanka had written to him. He gently ran his fingers over the bunch of envelopes, picked out one and asked me to open it. It was a letter of gratitude from Charumathi, thanking him for resolving a family issue.

Then, he asked me to open some of the other envelopes and give him the letters.

Looking at one of the letters he asked Swamiji, 'You can read Tamil, isn't it?'

Swamiji began reading the letter aloud.

Respected Gurudev,

I am Tamilselvan, Political Secretary of the LTTE. I am writing to you in my personal capacity now. I write this letter in complete secrecy. It is with a heavy heart that I write about my disappointment that I could not receive you with honour when you came to our Tamil motherland. I strongly feel, for us, this was a last missed chance for peace.

Our leader was reluctant to meet you as he was misguided by some of the senior aides. I personally believe you can still help resolve the situation and bring dignity and honour back to the Tamils of Sri Lanka. I have read some of your books, your ideas are liberating. This should help our liberation struggle. Our leader did not take my advice and it hurts me. I cannot talk to you via satellite phone also.

This letter is from me to you purely on a personal level and not in any official capacity. But I firmly believe, as you are a spiritual leader, I feel you are the only person who can give us freedom in the true sense. All our Peace initiatives have failed. Please tell me how can we convince our leader Prabhakaran to bring final success to our long Tamil struggle?

Gurudev was surprised to receive such a letter, a truly shocking one.

I told Gurudev, 'Tamilselvan has been the face of most of the peace talks that had taken place from 2002 onwards till now. But there is no way we can verify that this [letter] was written by him. This could be a hoax.'

Gurudev kept silent. But I could feel behind the silence that the master's mind was seeing something I couldn't. He told me, 'Ask Sameer to come with the camera at 11 a.m. tomorrow.'

I wondered what he was up to.

Sameer was the key cameraperson who had seen Gurudev from behind the lens for several years, recording and sharing with the world every audio and video that one may have seen of Gurudev till date.

Next morning, Sameer's team set up the camera in the Badri Vishala meeting room and was ready to roll. Swamiji and I were waiting. We had absolutely no clue about what Gurudev's plan was. Our tension mounted with each passing moment, only to ease upon his arrival.

Gurudev articulated his message for Prabhakaran, impressing upon him that violence would not lead to any success and that his goal should be pursued through peaceful means.

He then told Sameer to copy the message on a few CDs and hand them over to Swamiji and me. He asked us to get them delivered into the 'tiger's den' as soon as possible.

A day later, we left for Colombo and began the task of handing over the confidential CDs to some of our contacts, who we knew would ensure that they reached Prabhakaran soon.

We didn't hear from anyone in the LTTE or from their agents. Perhaps they were too busy to even think of peace.

~

By mid-2007, the Sri Lankan government had seized most of the LTTE-controlled areas in the eastern part of the country, which included the districts of Trincomalee, Batticaloa and Ampara.

The Mavil Aaru episode had ignited the government to keep the Tamil rebels fully engaged in the eastern sector, after which its focus shifted to attacking the northern areas of Tamil territories.

One August evening, Reverend Sister Consilia, a Catholic nun from the Holy Cross Convent, called me saying that she wanted to meet me while I was in Colombo. A hop, skip and jump, and she was at my door. At sixty-five years and after thirty years of teaching English to school and college students, she still woke up at 4 a.m. to practise the padma sadhana (series of yoga postures) and sudarshan kriya.

'They keep me going and give me the strength to handle today's generation,' she told me, handing over a big bag bursting with a variety of fruit, biscuits, a bottle of strawberry jam and prunes. She would hand me a goody bag every time we met, playing Santa Claus.

'It's my duty to take care of you, when you are doing Gurudev's holy work in our country,' she would often tell me. Being a nun for over twenty-five years, she knew what it was to serve society selflessly.

In learning about Gurudev's teachings, her spiritual quest had finally found an anchor. She was in great awe of him and would sit for hours listening to me talk about his work, life and wisdom. She admired the qualities of Jesus in him, which inspired her to write an awesome book, *The Spirit Blows Where It Wills*.

Once she told me that she also came to see me to listen to my unique style of English, where I unrepentantly break many rules of grammar! While I thought she would rap me on the knuckles as the teacher she was, fortunately my talk and tenor found favour with her.

That evening, she broached the idea of her desire to become an Art of Living teacher to help spread Gurudev's knowledge among the people of Sri Lanka, especially the Tamils. Thus, she became the first Asian Catholic nun to teach the Art of Living programme.

Just then, I received Gurudev's call from India. He asked me to go to Jaffna immediately and conduct trauma-relief programmes as the war had now slowly but definitely reached the northern region.

Sister Consilia offered to get me accommodation for a few days in her home town Jaffna even as she hoped that a few novice nuns learnt some basics of yoga and meditation.

The following night, I was on my way to Jaffna with just two sets of clothes and bags of milk powder and biscuits for children. Food, grocery and medicine shortages had become rampant, and the cost of living had increased due to the raging battle.

One weekend evening, as I was taking trauma-relief classes, the windows and doors rattled due to a massive sound. I thought it was an earthquake.

We all ran out of the room to see the sky light up due to rockets fired by the Lankan military into the LTTE-controlled areas a few kilometres away. I had never seen such a sight before. Someone told me that about twenty rockets could be launched in just a few seconds.

Everyone there had opinions on arms and war, as they had seen more than enough since childhood.

'This is now a new normal for us,' said a student as we resumed the yoga session even as another massive round of rockets blasted across the Jaffna skyline.

Here I was in the real theatre of war!

I began to distribute bags of milk powder and biscuits for children that I had carried from Colombo. Sylvia stood last in the queue to receive them. She sobbed like crazy and so did a few others.

The following week, the army asked all foreigners to leave Jaffna as fighting had intensified. I booked my ticket for Colombo, though I had a Sri Lanka resident visa. The army official reiterated that they would not take responsibility for any untoward happenings considering that I was not a Lankan citizen.

It appeared that a military settlement of the conflict had the upper hand rather than a political one.

~

On 2 January 2008, I was surprised by the official collapse of the much-touted six-year-old Ceasefire Agreement (CFA). The government had withdrawn from the CFA, alleging that the LTTE had violated it over 10,000 times. Just then, Swamiji called me from India to help put together a list of invitees for an international conference to be held in Oslo, Norway.

Gurudev continued his efforts at fostering peace in Sri Lanka, in spite of some unsuccessful attempts. He was not one to give up easily on things, especially when it involved the lives and deaths of thousands of people.

The following day, I discussed with Swamiji the specifics of the Norway conference and the delegate list, which included representatives from the Government of Sri Lanka, the LTTE, Tamil members of Parliament and religious leaders.

It was important that all key stakeholders and influencers in the conflict were represented well in the Conference on Peace and Reconciliation in South Asia held in April 2008.

The LTTE did not send any of its key leaders as they were engaged in the raging battle.

The three-day conference saw a gamut of ideas from delegates of several countries. Norway, which had brokered the now defunct CFA between the Sri Lankan government and the LTTE in 2002, was represented by Jon Hanssen-Bauer, who played a key role as peace envoy to Sri Lanka from 2006 until the end of war.

While the delegates discussed the ethnic strife in Sri Lanka in detail, the internal armed conflicts in Myanmar, Nepal and India were also in the spotlight.

India's insurmountable challenge of reigning in the Naxal rebels in some parts of the country had consumed hearts and minds at the conference.

The conference concluded, calling upon all stakeholders to opt for peaceful means and restraint while dealing with their respective situations.

Later, Gurudev also met with Erik Solheim, the Norwegian peace envoy who had a deep interest in the affairs of the Sri Lankan Tamils and had spearheaded the entire mediation process with the Sri Lankan government.

In January 2009, Oslo-based Professor Ole Danbolt Mjøs, the chairperson of the Nobel peace committee, came forward to invite Gurudev to Tromsø University, where he also served as senior faculty in physiology.

An interesting fact about that part of the North Pole is that the sun doesn't rise there from November to January. This phenomenon of the sun remaining below the horizon is called the polar night.

The 'Norwegian sun' had refused to shine.

The professor regretted that the Nobel peace committee had failed to acknowledge the contributions of Mahatma Gandhi by not conferring on him the Nobel Peace Prize many decades ago.

So he installed a beautifully sculpted bust of Gandhi on his university campus, where he took Gurudev to offer tribute.

Gurudev met a small and lively group of Sri Lankan Tamils there. The group thanked him for his proactive initiatives towards peace in their homeland.

In his speech in the evening, the professor lauded Gurudev's peace work and duly honoured him as the 'new Gandhi'.

14

Guns Become Roses

Gurudev, Swamiji and I landed by helicopter in Mandapam, a village in Tamil Nadu's Rameswaram, on 26 January 2009, a day celebrated in India as Republic Day. Several hundred people received us at the playground at noon.

Alighting from the chopper, we drove for a few minutes to arrive at a small patch of barren land adjoining a row of dilapidated low-cost houses that housed the Sri Lankan refugees who had been flowing in illegally from Sri Lanka every year over the last forty years.

It was an open secret that refugees living in this camp had been through immense hardship for decades due to several restrictions. While they engaged in daily-wage jobs like carpentry, masonry, etc., and earned a pittance, it was compulsory for them to return to the camp by 6 p.m.

A stack of permits from various levels of government officials had to be obtained by these refugees if they wanted to travel outside the village. Apparently, most approvals never come through.

Life as a refugee is not what you and I think it is. It's not just about receiving dinner and the dole.

A makeshift stage had been erected by the camp inmates and some of our volunteers to facilitate Gurudev's visit. Hundreds of them had lined up to meet him.

I stood on the left side of the stage where Santhan was speaking to another man in a typical Jaffna Tamil accent. In that same accent, I asked him when he had arrived in the camp.

He was all of fifteen when his family sold off all their jewellery to pay some fisherfolk who were willing to transport them by boat from Point Pedro on the northern coast of Sri Lanka to Rameswaram. In 1994, the war had thrown them into a deep financial crisis. It was then that they hatched this midnight plan to escape to India.

The arduous boat journey finally saw Santhan and his family get caught by an Indian Coast Guard vessel patrolling the high seas. Intense questioning by the Tamil Nadu police and a seventy-two-hour detention in a quarantine facility took the wind out of their sails.

Since then, his family had been living in poverty. They received meagre financial support and dry rations monthly from the Indian government.

Intelligence officials and the police kept a very close watch on the camp and the movements of its inmates as many had managed to escape and work in the black economy that brought them some money.

It was a known fact that some children who had escaped from the camp had landed in the hands of garment manufacturers, who exploited their helplessness and made them work in pathetic conditions for long hours for a very paltry income.

Gurudev stood on the stage in the camp in that noon sunshine and reiterated his demand for granting Indian citizenship to Sri Lankan refugees. He had earlier initiated a massive signature campaign to enlist public support and urge the Indian government to speed up the process.

In several countries around the world, refugees are ostensibly granted citizenship after a period of five years. Unfortunately, the Lankan refugees in India had no hopes of becoming Indian citizens even after thirty to forty years of living in these squalid camps.

It was rather ironical since some of those refugees were Tamils of Indian origin whose forefathers had been taken to Sri Lanka to work as labourers on tea estates.

Gurudev spent over an hour talking to the refugees, who spoke openly about their plight in the camps. Among them were some well-educated people who had undertaken illegal boat journeys to run away from the difficult circumstances on their island.

A few months later, Gurudev called on Manmohan Singh, the then Indian prime minister, and Pratibha Patil, the president, to highlight the plight of the refugees and to urge them to expedite the citizenship pleas of over 65,000 refugees languishing in various camps all over Tamil Nadu.

The Citizenship (Amendment) Act (CAA), 2019, passed in the Indian Parliament, does not consider Sri Lankan Tamils eligible for citizenship since they are seen as refugees due to ethnic issues rather than a persecuted religious group.

~

Kilinochchi had already been taken by the Sri Lankan military in a deadly battle in January 2009. The writing was on the wall.

The entire town was deserted, with civilians moving deep into the neighbouring Mullaitivu district along with LTTE cadres. As a sign of anger and vengeance, the cadres blew up a water tower while leaving so as to deprive the Sri Lankan forces of water.

It was just a matter of time before the war ended, with even the man on the street predicting it openly now.

I returned to India two months later, in March 2009, when Gurudev asked us to meet with some people and update them on our work in Sri Lanka.

New Delhi was already warm in March that year. Swamiji and I were in the corridors of power—the South Block. We met a brilliant official heading the Sri Lanka desk at the Union Ministry of External Affairs.

He received a big fat file. 'This is a report of all our work in Sri Lanka,' said Swamiji.

'What's your take on the situation unfolding there now?' he asked in a very concerned tone. However, everyone knew by now that the situation was veering towards a military settlement.

'The humanitarian crisis is quite serious. Food, drinking water and medical aid are in short supply,' Swamiji replied.

We had a brief chat about our Art of Living work there, when he suddenly said, 'Sir is calling us.'

M.K. Narayanan, the powerful national security adviser, welcomed us into his office. We handed him a copy of our work and experiences in Sri Lanka.

'We all favoured a political situation there within a united Sri Lanka . . . look where it has gone now,' remarked the elderly, erudite bureaucrat.

The war situation had by now already reached a point of no return. We concluded our meeting and left for a devotee's house in Delhi's Defence Colony.

The following afternoon, Preethi, a devotee from Sri Lanka, messaged me from Colombo, 'Our [the Sri Lankan] cricket team has been attacked in Lahore. Looks like a terror attack.'

Swamiji and I were in front of a television, watching visuals of the breaking news. Cricket celebrities from around the world were expressing their shock and sadness.

It had happened.

For several years, the cricket teams of New Zealand, Australia and India were reluctant to play in Pakistan due to frequent terrorist attacks. After hectic parleys, the Sri Lankan team finally agreed to play in Pakistan after their government persuaded them and offered to provide tight security on the lines accorded to the president of the country.

The Lankan team left their hotel in Lahore to play at the famous Gaddafi Stadium. As the bus reached Liberty Square, twelve armed terrorists began firing at its wheel.

The Lankan players didn't realize what had hit them and ducked down, with some of them lying down in the aisle. The Pakistan police fired at the terrorists, while the bus driver continued to drive at a high speed to somehow enter the stadium gates, which happened to be just 500 metres away.

However, this did not deter the terrorists from throwing a grenade under the bus, which exploded seconds after the bus drove over it.

The attackers also fired a rocket at the bus. The rocket missed the bus and hit an electric pole nearby. The driver of a minivan behind the bus, who was part of the cricket team's convoy, was killed instantly. The umpires, managers and other officials escaped with injuries after a security personnel got into the van and drove it to safety.

After the nearly ten-minute exchange of fire, the attackers ran to their motorcycles on the street and escaped. Six policemen and two civilians had died in the episode.

By now, the Lankan team was safely huddled inside the stadium, though a few players were injured in the melee. The psychological impact of the incident must have been tremendous on the team.

Pakistan air force helicopters flew into the stadium and airlifted the entire team immediately to the airport for their special flight back to Sri Lanka.

The LTTE was the first suspect but their spokesperson vehemently denied their involvement.

Later investigations revealed that the attack was masterminded by outlawed militant groups based in Pakistan.

This reinforced Pakistan's image and status as a terrorist haven.

As the whole world watched these shocking images on television, I told Swamiji that we should do something about it.

'What's your plan?' Swamiji asked me.

'I will leave for Colombo . . . Instead of coming to Bangalore . . . I will go to Chennai and take the morning flight,' I replied.

He immediately spoke to the Sri Lankan president and offered our assistance in trauma relief. President Mahinda Rajapaksa was well aware of our expertise in that field.

'I am very glad to hear it. Let's work it out,' the president said on a thankful note.

I called my father from Chennai airport at midnight, 'I just arrived from Delhi . . . am sleeping at the airport . . . have a 6 a.m. flight to Colombo . . . need to go on urgent work.' I was supposed to stay with my parents for two weeks since I had not seen them for almost two years.

'Travel is in your DNA,' laughed my long-retired sailor dad.

That morning at 10, I went to meet Dr Geethanjana Mendis, the famous sports-medicine expert, at the Institute of Sports Medicine on the other side of the Sri Lanka cricket headquarters.

'The president's office told me of you people . . . [Thilan] Samaraweera and Ajantha [Mendis] are in hospital . . . but out of danger. Some need trauma counselling . . . their family members also, maybe,' he said, offering me special Sri Lankan tea.

'I will talk to our boys and we can fix the session for trauma relief soon,' Dr Mendis reiterated his keen interest. He took me across the road to meet the team's physiotherapist.

Muttiah Muralitharan, the famous Sri Lankan spin bowler, was working out at the gym when I was introduced to the physiotherapist.

'He's from the Art of Living and they're going to offer trauma relief breathing exercises to all,' Dr Mendis told him.

'The Art of Living . . . a big name. Would love to learn,' the physiotherapist said, punching a fist in the air.

Hearing this, Muralitharan smiled at me as he took a break from the weights. He joined our conversation saying, 'Nice . . . looking forward.' We shook hands and he excused himself along with his physiotherapist for their routine workout session.

A few days later, Swamiji and I finalized the training schedule in a meeting with Dr Mendis. He offered us some lemon biscuits when I told him, 'Sir . . . No wonder your office is so fresh, bright, lime and lemony.'

He giggled like a baby. He had become a friend.

Dr Mendis spoke of his close association with Indian cricket champions, including Sunil Gavaskar, Sachin Tendulkar, Dilip Vengsarkar and others.

He also requested us to visit the hospital that evening and assess the psychological impact on the injured players, Ajantha Mendis and Tharanga Paranavitana.

A week later I walked up to the top floor, just above Dr Mendis' office, at 9 a.m. I wanted to be sure that all was fine with the arrangements made for the Sri Lankan cricket team to be comfortable as they learnt sudarshan kriya, yoga and meditation.

At the stroke of 10 a.m., the lift doors opened and Kumar Sangakkara walked in. I was in that small room opposite the mini auditorium.

'No one has come yet?' he asked me. 'You are the first . . . always,' I replied.

He laughed and I introduced myself. 'How do I address you?' I asked him.

'Call me Sanga!' he said in a real cool style.

He now went near the window to look down and said, 'Oh . . . our guys are still coming.'

I looked down too and saw the other players ambling slowly from the Sri Lanka Cricket board office.

I could also see a few schoolchildren wave at the players as they were crossing the road.

Sanga said, 'If this was India . . . those students would have grabbed them for pictures and autographs . . . In Sri Lanka no one bothers us.'

I laughed and told him, 'When I came to Sri Lanka in December 2004 . . . four youths saw me at Majestic Mall and thought I was Anil Kapoor [a popular Bollywood actor] and harangued me for an autograph!'

Sanga was in splits. 'What did you do then?' he asked. 'I had to rush out of the mall,' I quipped.

He revealed, 'Most times in India . . . I can't go out shopping quietly on my own . . . they mob me.'

Sanga's simplicity, charm and elegance left a mark on me that day. These qualities 'hat-tricked' the perfect gentleman in him.

Mahela Jayawardene, Muralitharan, Chaminda Vaas and the rest of the team started trooping into the hall, when Sanga told them, 'Hey guys, let's be on time. This is a very crucial training for us. They have something special for us to make us feel relaxed and energized.'

Swamiji walked in and I requested Sanga to introduce his teammates. We could sense shades of curiosity, deep anticipation and excitement on their faces.

A whole gamut of breathing exercises was taught to the team. They shared their unique experiences. For many, it was a refreshingly new beginning.

After the concluding session they all lined up for a photocall, which turned out to be a celebrative moment for all of us. We joked, laughed and danced to our heart's content. When everyone had left, Sanga came up to Swamiji and asked, 'I heard Gurudev went to meet Prabhakaran a few years ago. Sounds like a bold and daring initiative. What happened there?'

Swamiji shared the story over lunch.

~

I was in awe of the shiny, jet-black helicopter at the Ministry of Defence campus in Colombo. It was late in April 2009. Gurudev, Swamiji, a few others and I were getting ready to fly to a destination we had never seen before.

This was yet another turning point for me during my stay in Sri Lanka. The civil war was in its final phase and aerial bombings had scorched the earth. The Lankan military had created 'no-fire zones' for the thousands of civilians trapped in LTTE-held villages.

Our pilot told us that army helicopters had dropped leaflets urging people to quickly move from their village to refugee camps in the government-controlled Vavuniya district. Special safe passages and paths were created by military personnel for civilians to reach these camps.

However, many civilians chose to stay back in the 'no-fire zones'. A perfect evacuation plan was in place but casualties were also very high.

Many activists and international governments protested against the bombing and strafing that indiscriminately targeted the 'no-fire zones' with makeshift emergency clinics and hospitals. The Sri Lankan government vehemently denied this allegation.

We landed at the air force base in north-central Sri Lanka. Except for the loud drone of the helicopter that resonated with the sonic sounds of a war machine, there was a certain silence in the helicopter throughout the journey.

A humanitarian crisis was unfolding.

There was an air of hectic activity, with hundreds of uniformed personnel swarming the area. After the mandatory security checks, we immediately got into the waiting cars and rushed towards Vavuniya town.

After driving down a few kilometres, Gurudev suddenly noticed a huge open ground on the right side and asked for the car to be stopped.

We could see hundreds of people behind the barbed-wire fence. I quickly got out of the car and walked towards the heavily guarded local school premises, which had been converted into a makeshift refugee camp by the Sri Lankan armed forces.

A stout soldier stopped me and asked in Sinhalese, 'Who are you? Where are you from?'

I showed him a permission letter from the Ministry of Defence approving our visit to the refugee camps but he was sniffy about it.

He tossed the letter back into my hands and said in a stern voice, 'You can't go in.'

I asked him, 'Why? . . . we have the valid written permission from the MoD [Ministry of Defence].'

He again said, 'You cannot enter here. This letter is only for your travel to this province . . . not to enter refugee camps. The situation is serious. Please go away.'

I immediately tried calling the president's secretaries but none of them took my call. The sun was right above us, shining sharply. It must have been noon.

I saw the soldier tighten his grip on his gun as a show of authority as he pushed me lightly.

I countered his actions with a tough stare.

Suddenly, I noticed that the refugees had started to gather around a few hundred metres behind him. Many were waving and crying out aloud. They were obviously seeking help.

There was a peculiar frenzy in the air. For a moment, I thought the people would break into a riot.

The soldier quickly called a colleague and told him to tell the refugees to go back to their tents immediately. About a hundred white tents were pitched on the school grounds behind the buildings.

Now Gurudev got out of the car and walked towards the soldier. Pointing to the restless crowd behind, he said, 'Look . . . they are calling me.'

Without batting an eyelid, the soldier simply lowered his gun and respectfully stepped aside.

As Gurudev walked in, hundreds of refugees broke the security cordon from inside the camp and rushed towards him. The two soldiers watched the scene quietly even as other uniformed personnel looked bewildered.

A few refugees hugged Gurudev. Many broke into sobs and began to describe their woes.

He enquired about their well-being and living conditions.

A man sobbed loudly saying that he had lost his entire family the previous week. An elderly woman, clinging to her malnourished granddaughter, asked Gurudev for his help to find the girl's parents.

Another soldier came up to me and said, 'Let him address all the people via the public address system so that those still inside the camp can benefit by listening to him.'

The public address system was already in place for soldiers to give routine instructions to the camp inmates.

As Gurudev took hold of the microphone and started talking, hundreds of more people came rushing from inside the camp.

The army personnel were baffled.

The soldier who had stopped us earlier came up to me and asked, 'Who is he? These refugees don't even seem to know him and yet they are clinging to him.'

It seemed as though the sun had melted his heart. Guns became roses.

I continued listening to Gurudev address the people, 'I am here to help you. Don't worry. You will all be quickly resettled in your villages. Have faith and confidence.'

A thousand people heaved a sigh of relief and clapped.

Just as Gurudev was concluding his speech, I saw an armoured vehicle approach the school gate. A seemingly senior army officer got out of it and rushed into the camp with ten heavily armed security personnel.

Introducing himself as Colonel Induneel, he said, 'Welcome, your holiness. Everyone here needs your blessings.' He explained to us that while they had received information from the MoD on our visit, the details hadn't reached the soldiers at the refugee camps. He informed us that approximately seventy thousand refugees had crossed over the previous night from the war zone to the camps.

Then, he offered to accompany us to the Menik Farm sector, a few kilometres away, which was divided into different zones for ease of management.

A few weeks earlier, large tracts of forest land outside Vavuniya town had been cleared by the Sri Lankan government to establish these camps for the thousands of people coming in from the war zone, as the final offensive against the LTTE was in full swing.

We drove on the highway, following the colonel's armoured vehicle, towards the next sector. Along the way, we noticed hordes of refugees communicating animatedly with each other. They were separated by a barbed wire fence.

The scorching noon heat was heightened by their wails of utter despair.

Gurudev asked for the car to be stopped. He pointed to the crowds and told me, 'Look . . . look at the misery.' I broke down. We were witnessing first-hand the pain and suffering caused by war. He then asked me to clarify with the army official on what we had seen. In two minutes, we reached the main entrance of Chettikulam camp where hundreds of refugees were milling around.

I got out of the car and quickly ran up to the colonel to ask him about the groups of people talking across the barbed fence. He told me that the army had devised a mechanism for the refugees to register the names of their missing relatives.

He added that prior appointments were being allotted to the refugees to meet with their traced relatives, some of whom would usually be found in adjoining camps among the several thousand displaced people.

He also shared that they had confirmed information about many LTTE cadres, including potential suicide bombers, infiltrating groups of civilians fleeing the war zone into these camps. Therefore, the military officials had no option but to carefully screen and profile people for verification and conduct interrogations if required.

I briefed Gurudev accordingly on what we had witnessed while driving along the highway.

~

Our car now entered another camp when hundreds came running and surrounded it. For several years, having been displaced by war and shifting from place to place, they were used to seeing vehicles of aid organizations like the UN, Red Cross, UNICEF, etc.

Perhaps they were wondering what our black four-wheel drive was doing in their camp.

Gurudev, who was seated in the front passenger seat, quickly rolled down the window and stretched out his hand to the people.

A middle-aged man clutched his palm and cried, 'I was a flourishing businessman with rice mills. We are now reduced to beggars with not even proper rice to eat.'

Many others interrupted him to share their agony and distress with Gurudev. Some women wailed at the loss of their dear ones as they didn't know if they had gone missing or were dead.

Gurudev showed unfailing interest in each one of them, asking them to speak one at a time.

A schoolteacher told him how in spite of the difficult circumstances in the camp she continued to gather children from the tents and teach them lessons each day under the shade of trees.

Gurudev spoke with a few more people, some of whom were doctors and the others well-educated individuals with flourishing careers who had lost it all now.

Swamiji and I were expecting to see Deepa here but all the faces we saw seemed new, tired and worn out. An elderly man told Swamiji that hundreds of people had walked long distances without food and even waded through water to escape the bombing and strafing. Swamiji held his hand and consoled him.

Here we were in the back seat, witnessing this living hell, when two children suddenly asked Swamiji if he had any biscuits. I was shaken to see the hunger in their eyes.

He quickly got out of the car and took them to a truck behind us. We had sent a few trucks in advance with the help of our local volunteers in Vavuniya town. It was filled to the brim with dry rations and clothes.

A swarm of about five hundred people came rushing to the truck and the children disappeared. Swamiji told the crowd, 'Please stand in a line. All these materials are for you. Everyone will receive them.' The entire time his eyes kept searching for those children.

His voice drowned in the mild chaos.

In a minute, I saw Gurudev walk towards Swamiji and climb on the truck to start distributing the relief material. The sultry summer did not deter him from continuing to distribute the relief materials for over an hour.

Swamiji took a packet and went searching for those kids. He wanted to give them the biscuits from the dry ration kit. Soon, he spotted them seated near a tent close by.

Tears rolling down his bony cheeks, one of the boys told him, 'Look at those people, they pushed us behind. They are not even bothered about us children.' Swamiji took a biscuit and fed the boy, as he gently stroked his head and comforted him, shifting his attention to the joy of that moment.

I heard repeated announcement of names through the public address system. I wondered what had happened. I recalled what the colonel had told me about the 'track-and-meet' system for identifying missing persons.

The second truck bearing the relief materials was now empty. We all left for the next camp called Kadirgamar. This camp housed around forty Hindu priests, who complained about the lack of water.

As these camps were established on an emergency basis, providing basic amenities to the unending flow of refugees, in a very short span of time, was a huge challenge. A government official shared his woes with me, as Gurudev was speaking with the priests.

As per tradition, these priests ate their first meal only after a bath and prayer. Shortage of water had prevented them from carrying out their daily rites and rituals. This had become the cause for a deep grouse.

We took the road back to the Vavuniya air force base just before sunset, when we had to fly back to Colombo. A meeting with President Mahinda Rajapaksa was on the cards.

Gurudev suggested to the president that he should try to improve the living conditions of the refugees, while facilitating resettlement in their homes. Gurudev also sought the early release of priests, senior citizens and the differently abled persons from the camps.

After the war was over and some villages cleared of debris, these categories of people were among the first to be released in phases.

Gurudev left for India two days later, on 23 April. I felt a massive vacuum in the wake of his departure.

As the images and emotions of the day flashed in my mind, deep down I felt that this was not my last visit to these camps.

15

Jayalalithaa and the White Flag

I was more than familiar with Chennai summer but this season was different, as election campaigning soared with each passing day, just like the war across the southern seas.

The day of the state elections, 13 May 2009, was three weeks away. I observed politicians across the board spewing their favourite rhetoric, lines and rhymes in support of the Sri Lankan Tamil cause.

Each political party tried its best to outdo the other. They organized relay fasts, protests and raucous processions to express their deep anguish over the raging war. I even went to one of the protest sites, where a man shared with me the inside story of how he was 'hired' for a paltry sum of Rs 100 along with a sumptuous breakfast thrown in before he sat on the hunger strike! His so-called 'fast' would conclude at

9 p.m., after which he would be given a dinner takeaway. I wasn't surprised over these age-old tactics. He shared that many of his friends and relatives were having a field day, thanks to the election campaigning.

I had just finished counselling a woman on the phone who wanted a solution to her life's trauma. She sought help to handle her second husband, who was a workaholic. She claimed that her first husband was an alcoholic.

After her rant, she asked for an instant solution. It was then that Swamiji's number flashed on my phone.

It was breaking news. He and Gurudev would be landing in Chennai the following day.

I was taken by surprise because Gurudev, Swamiji and I had arrived together from Colombo just a few days earlier and Gurudev had addressed a press conference at the Chennai Press Club to highlight his visit to the Vavuniya relief camps.

Absolutely no one knew that he was coming back to Chennai. It was a closely guarded secret. We drove to Poes Garden, one of the poshest localities of the city, that evening.

Our car entered the residence of J. Jayalalithaa, the former chief minister of Tamil Nadu. She had extended an invitation to Gurudev after hearing about his recent visit to the refugee camps.

She told us that she had just returned from a whirlwind tour of many districts to campaign for her party's candidates. There was not an iota of fatigue, boredom or inertia in her disposition when I saw her enter the meeting room. I was mighty impressed with her, just as impressed as I was with her hit films in the late 1970s, when she ruled the world of films as an accomplished actor.

She asked curiously if Gurudev had any videos from his recent Lanka visit.

I flipped open the laptop to ready the 'the theatre' for her, while Gurudev and Jayalalithaa carried on their conversation. She remained engrossed in the video, which highlighted the living conditions and the collective psyche behind the barbed-wire relief camps. All along, I noticed that she was not only a good listener but a keen observer as well, imbibing every word and sentiment from the video.

She was moved after watching it and her eyes were moist.

Gurudev then told her he had spoken to President Rajapaksa to ensure that all displaced people were settled quickly in their towns and villages now that the war had culminated.

After a brief chat, she asked him, 'What is the point of being good?' Gurudev looked at her in surprise.

She quoted examples from the famous epics of the Ramayana and the Mahabharata. She stated that Yudhishtir was a good man but had suffered all his life while Duryodhana, who did evil things, enjoyed, made merry on earth and still went to heaven after his death. Even Ravana, despite his behaviour, was liberated in the end, whereas Lord Ram, despite being righteous, went through trials and tribulations for the most part of his life. Jayalalithaa added that during her tenure as chief minister, she had made Tamil Nadu number one on several fronts. However, she lamented the performance of the government of the day, saying that good governance had taken a back seat.

Then, she reiterated her question, 'If this is the case, what's the point of being a good person?'

We were all surprised at this question. It seemed as though she was trying to draw Gurudev into an argument. However, he has the unique skill of not being lured into polemics. He quickly brought her attention back to the main theme of the discussion.

After the hour-long meeting, it looked like there was a perceptible shift in her attitude towards the Sri Lankan Tamils. She saw us off at the main door.

Before we even reached the house where Gurudev was to stay that night, her famous television channel, Jaya TV, flashed a news item decrying the plight of the Tamils in the island nation.

I was surprised to note that her call for an independent Tamil state in Sri Lanka had now resurfaced.

~

Sri Lanka was the cynosure of all eyes that day in May 2009. Thousands of civilians were trapped in an area of around 3 km in Mullivaikkal, with the deep sea on one side and the vigorously advancing Lankan military on the other side. The chariots of war were already speeding in sixth gear towards that small strip of land in the north-east, where Prabhakaran and a few top aides were cornered. Intense aerial bombing and shelling had pushed these civilians into that final battle zone.

During this week, all the people who had placed obstacles in Gurudev's way, while he tried to resolve the Sri Lankan Tamil issue, now requested his help to stop the war at any cost. Politicians, human rights activists, LTTE sympathizers and non-resident Tamils based abroad were among them.

In the last week of April, Gurudev left for Europe for his scheduled public tour of discourse and meetings. Considering his body of work in conflict resolution, the Norwegian University of Life Sciences had invited him to receive an honorary doctorate.

Norway, a small but beautiful country with a huge appetite for peace, has been at the forefront of many peace initiatives around the world.

From declaring peace awards to proffering their good offices in helping bring peace in conflict-ridden zones and nations, the Norwegians are typically the first to play the role of the peacemaker.

Gurudev arrived in Oslo just a day before the event, when his secretary in Europe was informed that the doctorate Gurudev was supposed to receive was being withdrawn.

This news created a furore among a very large section of the academic community and peacemakers in Norway and other parts of Europe, leaving them shocked at the impropriety of it all.

But Gurudev remained unruffled.

By my reckoning, in accepting an award or title, it's the giver and the award itself that stand elevated and honoured. If you are to praise someone, it only reflects your goodness and higher qualities.

Meting out such unethical treatment to Gurudev only reflected the standing of the university's highest offices. Apparently, a few in the top management of the university felt completely helpless as two Left-wing professors staunchly opposed conferring a doctorate on an Indian spiritual guru.

Prejudice against gurus is an untold story.

Perhaps the Norwegian sun had not dawned on them, leaving them in the darkness of prejudice. When you are prejudiced, you go on listening in a selective way, imbibing things that only strengthen and support your own preconceptions, leaving you tightly closed.

Several members of that university were left hugely embarrassed and aghast at the injustice faced by Gurudev. Norway's penchant for peace and its credibility for peacemaking became vulnerable to questioning and criticism.

The prejudice that Mahatma Gandhi had experienced in many parts of the world still seemed to continue in its twenty-first-century version.

After the Norway visit, as Gurudev drove through Bern, Switzerland, his attention was caught by a huge group of Tamils demonstrating against the final phase of the Sri Lanka war.

He sent one of his assistants to invite them to the venue of his evening talk, where he urged them to convince their leader to come to terms with the ground realities.

On 2 May, Gurudev was in the Netherlands to discuss the details of a public programme with a group of European volunteers, when his phone rang. One of his assistants saw that it was an 'unknown number' and hesitated to attend to the call. It stopped ringing.

It rang once again. Gurudev looked at his assistant and asked him, 'Who is it?' Fred replied, 'Unknown.' To this, Gurudev retorted with his trademark wit, 'Be open to exploring the unknown.' The room exploded with laughter.

The caller's voice wasn't too clear for a few seconds and the call got disconnected.

In a few minutes, it rang again. A man said in Tamil, 'This is Nadesan, political chief of the LTTE, calling from Mullaitivu.'

Recognizing that it was an important call from a top LTTE leader, Gurudev walked into the adjoining room. It had been just over ten days since his return from the refugee camps for the internally displaced people.

By this time, much death and destruction had already happened.

Since a lot of screaming and sounds of blasts could be heard in the caller's background, Gurudev asked him, 'What's happening? What is the situation there now?'

Nadesan said in a trembling voice, 'We made a very big mistake by not receiving you. We should have met you when you came to our motherland.'

Nadesan regretted it.

He added that over 1,60,000 people in Mullaitivu were facing acute shortage of food and medical supplies. The only hospital there had been bombed, and twenty-two children had died. Nadesan expressed the LTTE's readiness for any kind of settlement with a third party other than the Sri Lankan army.

Gurudev replied that their request would be communicated to the Sri Lanka government.

Considering the obedience that the LTTE cadres at every level had shown towards their leader, it was apparent that the call had been made at the behest of Prabhakaran.

Swamiji was in Beijing, keenly browsing Sri Lankan news websites that were giving regular updates on the last phase of the war. Suddenly, he saw Gurudev's number flash on his phone.

Swamiji began sharing the amazing experiences of some of the participants who had undertaken the advanced meditation programme that had just concluded that weekend.

Gurudev quickly drew his attention to the news that needed immediate response—the call that Nadesan had made from a satellite phone. Gurudev further instructed Swamiji to connect with the secretary of the Sri Lankan president to relay the LTTE's latest message.

Gurudev also told Swamiji that Nadesan would get in touch with him for further communication and that the humanitarian crisis had become unmanageable in Sri Lanka.

Given the gravity of the situation, Swamiji quickly drafted an email to the Lankan president's office.

Gurudev also connected with Vijay Nambiar, the then chef de cabinet of the UN, keeping him updated on the LTTE's messages and its willingness for any kind of settlement with a third party.

The following day, there were five missed calls from an unknown number on Swamiji's phone. Nadesan contacted him and once again insisted on securing the Sri Lankan government's guarantee of a ceasefire and a settlement with a third party.

Swamiji understood Nadesan's desperation, as the army was already at the LTTE's doorstep. The clock was ticking away and every second felt crucial.

President Mahinda Rajapaksa called Gurudev and informed him that he wouldn't be able to stop the war at this stage as it had gone beyond a point of no return and it would bring down the morale of his soldiers. He added in an upbeat tone that they were almost there, nearing victory, and that they had to end this terror that had been terrorizing everyone for many years. He was ready to grant amnesty to the surrendering LTTE cadres. According to protocol, they had to show a white flag signifying their willingness to surrender.

Swamiji communicated the same to Nadesan.

A flurry of messages and phone calls became the order of the day and even midnight, even as international attention was on the climax of this war.

A few days later, a local newspaper in Sri Lanka, mysteriously and mischievously, published a news article declaring that Gurudev was working out a ceasefire between the LTTE and the Sri Lankan government. This came as a shock to all of us as this news was false.

A senior government official asked us to deny the claim since the Sri Lankan president had already said that it was too late to stop the war.

Just like the lull before the storm, messages from the LTTE stopped completely. When I came to know of this, all I could do was pray for those people.

On 18 May, some TV channels declared that 'Nadesan, Pulidevan and a few other LTTE cadres were shot dead at point-blank range while surrendering'. Nadesan's wife, a Sinhalese, was also in the front line during their surrender.

There were media reports offering different versions, some claimed that Nadesan was shot dead by the LTTE cadres, while others claimed that the Sri Lankan military had executed him. No one knows what exactly happened that Monday morning.

Prabhakaran was killed a few hours later.

Thus ended the twenty-six-year Sri Lankan war on 18 May 2009. Now the moot question was: what lay ahead for the Tamil survivors and their future generations?

I called Gurudev on the night of 19 May, the day the war was officially declared over. I had a long chat with him, briefed him on the situation and then dropped my most cherished question of that time, 'So, I can now return to India for good?'

He replied, 'Your work starts now. Stay there for some time. Go back to the relief camps and give meditation sessions.'

Before going to bed, I recollected the evening of September 2004, a few months before Gurudev sent me to Sri Lanka.

Gurudev had called me to seek an update on various aspects of the ashram administration.

He stood clasping with his right hand an iron pole, connected to the high ceiling, in the centre of his simple and single-room accommodation of twenty-three years.

As I was briefing him, he started twirling in a circle around the pole, his body tilted outwards towards the floor, his loose hair swaying in the breeze that flowed through the small windows.

He reminded me of a child on a merry-go-round when he stopped exactly where I stood.

'There is no need to hide anything. Empty your cup and be free,' he told me.

He went on to twirl the second time and stopped next to me once again, saying, 'We have no private life. Just one life. Serve the people.'

After that phone call, I continued to stay in Sri Lanka. Not just for four weeks or four months but for four years.

16

The Bridge Flowed. The River Stopped

While massive celebrations marked the military's victory in the war, with the streets and homes of the Sinhalese lit up, a pall of gloom had descended on the Tamils, with many becoming apprehensive of their future.

I saw that the Sri Lankan government's success was celebrated and displayed in hundreds of households in Colombo, wherein people had placed the national flag in their balconies, and on the walls and gates. Raucous street parties replete with Baila dance and food became the order of the day.

Some of the Tamils I knew had made plans to emigrate to Western countries, while others had decided to stay on in the country and continue their battle politically.

The international community had raised concerns over the last stages of the war, with serious allegations of war crimes against both the LTTE and the Lankan military. This debate continues till date.

One warm afternoon in the last week of May, I received a call from the defence ministry. The caller said, 'Our officer wants to meet you. Please attend a meeting tomorrow. I will have an official invitation hand-delivered by this evening.'

The situation of the inmates in the relief camps needed attention. These people required more materials, resources and assistance on every front to keep them going till the army 'fully cleared' the areas ravaged by the war and permitted them to return to their homes. It was against this backdrop that we were invited to the meeting.

We were seated at a round table when the army officer said, 'I was told of Art of Living foundation's expertise in humanitarian relief work and trauma-relief programmes. Can you roll out your programmes for the displaced people in the camps?'

I told him that the president had already granted us permission to do so in April, when Gurudev had met with him, and that we were all set to implement our two-hour trauma-relief modules spread over four days.

The official asked me to submit immediately all details of the Art of Living volunteers and teachers who would be a part of this initiative so as to ensure smooth and secure implementation. A week after the meeting, our group was in Vavuniya.

We had a really huge task on our hands—to handle the mental health of almost 3,00,000 people. Each day we would travel from Vavuniya town to these camps, which were about 10 km away, and return late in the evening.

Hundreds of people seated in rows and columns would breathe to the sudarshan kriya rhythm of peace and tranquillity in separate batches every morning, afternoon and evening. The sessions were purely voluntary and made available to everyone.

There were many among the camp inmates, especially young people, who had lost a leg in landmine explosions but their strength and commitment saw them participate fully in our programme.

Spreading a thin piece of cloth on the rough sands, the people would sit and listen intently. Thanks to our daily visits, we had almost become a part and parcel of the camp.

I began exploring the camp, only to discover a government-owned bank, a supermarket, an outpatient department (OPD) clinic, a temple and a church. The bank allowed the refugees to receive remittance from their relatives abroad. The Tamils in Europe, the US and Canada were known to have generously supported their people back home by sending them hundreds of dollars every month.

I noticed small kitchen gardens with spinach, tomatoes and chillies, springing up outside the tin-roof shelters and tents. These for me symbolized the powerful 'never say die' spirit of the refugees. Flooding due to sewage water, and many cases of jaundice, diarrhoea and fever were a daily feature in the camp. What we thought of as a temporary relief camp had slowly transformed into a village over a few weeks. I wondered if the refugees' stay was going to be prolonged now, delaying their resettlement.

I had the chance to interact with several people. One morning after the meditation and yoga session, a young woman clad in a blue shirt and red skirt walked up to me.

'I got amazing relief from the stress that I was going through. I wish I had learnt the sudarshan kriya earlier,' she said with a smile. I had seen her sitting in the front row every day during the four-day session.

The time I had spent here was an eye-opener for me on how life can throw up surprises and shock one to the bones. It can throw a man from riches to rags, home to exile and freedom to captivity.

I looked at the barbed-wire fence surrounding the camp and wondered if there was a very thin line between heaven and hell.

A few months into delivering the trauma-relief programmes at the camp, a young man in a multicoloured sarong stopped me just as I was about to leave for lunch. He told me that he wanted to chat with me in private. I was hungry, so I suggested that we meet after lunch.

'I am Deepa's brother,' he shot back in a gruff voice.

I asked him if he was referring to Deepa from Jaffna. He confirmed the same with a heavy nod and my hunger evaporated. I held his hand and asked him eagerly, 'Where is Deepa?'

He bowed his head and stood quiet for a few seconds. He quickly led me to his squalid tin-roofed dormitory and made me sit beside him. I could feel a sense of urgency and insecurity in him when he told me that he did not want any soldiers to see us together.

I wondered if I shouldn't hear what he was going to say next, since I had already heard enough personal and collective horror stories describing the last stages of the war from many others in the camp.

But how could I not hear about our very own Deepa, who was not only a volunteer but was almost family to all of us.

Thambi's lips quivered as he recalled the sequence of events.

In the second week of May, Deepa and he were in a village in Puthukkudiyiruppu town, where the Sri Lankan army had cornered several thousand people.

The army used megaphones urging the people to move along the main highway towards the key point of Vadduvakal bridge on Nay Aru in Mullaitivu, the LTTE-controlled district with white beaches tucked away in the north-east corner of Sri Lanka.

Thousands of people had finally decided to leave the last patch of the war zone. Many LTTE cadres had chosen to quietly drop their weapons, change into civilian clothes and merge with the fleeing civilians.

They had perhaps already realized that the war was closing in on them, whether they wished it or not.

However, heavy firing and shelling on both sides continued, frequently leading to the death of the displaced civilians.

Many of them were fired at by the LTTE cadres as they started moving out in batches, Thambi reiterated.

Several others with whom I had interacted with separately in the camp had told me the same story. Apparently, the cadres shot their own people in the legs in order to stop them from escaping.

I asked Thambi, 'Why would they do that?'

He replied, 'This was to keep the civilians as human-shields to surround the area where the top LTTE leaders were in hiding. This was also done to buy time for their clandestine escape. Anyways, the Sri Lankan military firing on civilians would have become a human rights issue. This siege continued for several days.'

Deepa and her brother were crossing the Vadduvakal bridge.

They had never seen thousands of people walk shoulder to shoulder though every step forward felt like a dead march. Loud cries, complaints and curses rent the air.

Most of these people had not eaten, taken medicines or slept with a roof over their heads in the days prior to reaching this bridge.

Thambi added that Deepa turned her head back for a moment to look at the crowds behind her, when she saw the horrific sight of some men, women and children walking in tattered clothes.

Their souls bared, but the fire of hope still burning in them.

Weighed down by the deep sorrow and agony in her, one of the women was singing mournful tunes that added to the despair in the air. Deepa quickly unbuttoned her shirt and offered it to the woman, who was trying to cover her bleeding breasts with thin, shivering fingers.

Suddenly, Deepa felt that the bridge was moving with the multitudes of people walking aimlessly. Seeing hundreds of dead bodies in the water on either side gave her the feeling that the river was no more.

The stench was unbearable. There were eyes sticking out. Not one, but a hundred pairs. It seemed as though intestines were on display too. Sun-dried bloodstains stood out in the scorching heat.

Bags, clothes, cycles and other belongings that mark a journey, lay still in their tracks.

Thambi looked into my eyes and said that they had crossed this bridge on several occasions as children to visit their grandma to celebrate festivals or to simply spend time with her. She was their ancient love. He recollected her pretty wrinkles and her toothless mouth.

'Some teeth were for display but the others were to chew life's challenges,' he told me with a half-smile. 'She would have you for lunch if you took the pranks too far,' he reminisced.

Having crossed this stretch and walked for about a kilometre more, the siblings saw a few injured men lying down on the wayside and crying for help.

No one had anything to offer to them, other than prayers from a distance.

Some army officials asked everyone to continue walking and said that medical help for the injured was on its way. After another kilometre's crawl, Thambi and Deepa sat down for a few minutes to quench their thirst and satiate their hunger, with the army doling out water bottles and biscuits, before getting them to board the buses to relief camps in Vavuniya.

Deepa guzzled down the bottle of water and looked poignantly towards the bridge and said, 'If only our leader had discussed some solutions with Gurudev . . . we would not have had to see such a grim situation on this bridge.'

Thambi agreed.

Just then, a Lankan soldier grabbed Thambi and pushed him into a waiting bus. Deepa screamed while being packed off on another bus.

That was the last time Thambi saw Deepa.

Just as Thambi finished reliving the last moments of his time with Deepa, I saw a few people queuing up in the distance. I asked him what was happening there.

He explained that government officials were creating new profiles for each and everyone in the camp because they had lost their national identity cards while being shifted frequently from one place to the other, as the Lankan military fought through Tamil territory. It was also a skilful way of identifying LTTE cadres from among the civilians, as many of them had discarded their weapons and merged with the refugees flowing into the camps.

Though the war was over, the government did not want potential suicide bombers to sneak into Colombo and indulge in violence through their sleeper cells that ran deep in several parts of the island.

Thambi revealed that interrogation of varying degrees had apparently happened alongside the profiling exercise. These were conducted jointly by the government administrative staff, and military and intelligence officials.

As I wrote this chapter on 8 June 2021, I remembered all the lovely Tamils and Sinhalese who had shared with me their meager resources.

Whether it was sharing a few slices of bread, a bowl of rice, sleeping under a tin roof or on the cold floor.

No wonder, people refer to Sri Lanka as the teardrop-shaped pearl of the Indian Ocean. Considering all that they went through, these people still strive to shine.

17

Master Plan

No one entered the dormitory for a while, as everyone was busy waiting in serpentine queues for lunch.

Suddenly, Thambi hugged me and started crying inconsolably. I allowed him to express himself. The heat was piercing through the tin roof. I was soaked in sweat and Thambi's grief.

'She went missing. I know what must have happened to her but I just don't want to believe it. It gives me sleepless nights,' he cried.

For a second, my heart skipped a beat. With a lump in my throat, I asked, 'Why did she run away from home?'

'After Prabhakaran's Martyrs' Day speech in November 2006, the LTTE forced us to recruit more people . . . and also called back every cadre operating in various capacities across

Sri Lanka. So she came back to Kilinochchi. The war was to start. We were all in war-ready mode.'

I began to connect the dots and my head reeled. Oh gosh! Then who was Deepa?

Thambi said, 'Did you know she was sent to spy on you and Swamiji . . . your organization? She was one of our best spies ever.'

'But her life changed after she met Gurudev, when he offered her his food at the Kataragama temple guest house . . . She told me every single thing that happened there. She had great respect and gratitude for him.'

Thambi had made a seismic revelation.

The day before Gurudev had gone to Kilinochchi to meet Prabhakaran, Deepa was present at a crucial meeting with the LTTE leader and his top aides in a secret bunker. Among them were Tamilselvan, the political head, Nadesan, the head of the police wing, Pottu Amman, the intelligence chief, and a few others.

Many points of view flew across the room, punctuated by heated arguments.

Since a meeting between their leader and Gurudev had already been promised, Tamilselvan had insisted that it was not appropriate to pull out at the last minute.

Another aide disagreed and jumped to his feet saying that Gurudev could use his powers of persuasion to convince the LTTE cadres to give up arms totally. He puffed his chest and boasted of their military strength while declaring that they would win the war.

Some in the group felt that this was not the time for talks of any kind, as they presumed that Gurudev would talk about meditation and attempt to soften them with his hypnotic eyes.

Tamilselvan insisted that considering Gurudev's stature and goodwill in many parts of the world, allowing the meeting to happen would go a long way towards improving the LTTE's image on the global stage.

The intelligence head reminded his comrades that plans to take Gurudev hostage were already in place.

The discussion continued for a while and Prabhakaran left the room quietly. Tamilselvan seemed disappointed and walked away too.

I couldn't believe what Thambi was sharing. There was doubt in my mind and I asked him if I should trust him at all.

He quickly unbuttoned his chequered shirt and showed me a silver pendant tied to a black thread that hung around his neck.

I recalled Gurudev giving little coin-shaped silver pendants to everyone at the Kataragama temple guest house. Deepa was one of the recipients. In those days, he used to hand them out as a token of blessing.

'She gave it to me in the summer of 2007, saying that it would protect me,' Thambi recollected.

This silver pendant had now replaced the cyanide capsule that LTTE cadres normally wore around their necks. If they were captured alive, their trademark practice was to instantly bite 'the death pill' to avoid being tortured by their enemies.

Thambi continued sharing the inside story.

As soon as Prabhakaran and his aides left the bunker, Deepa asked the intelligence head for some time to chat.

She told him that they had made a very big mistake by not encouraging Prabhakaran to meet with Gurudev in Kilinochchi.

He snapped back saying that they didn't want to be softened like lambs since their goal was clearly to fight and win.

'And to top it all, how could you even think of kidnapping Gurudev? If you cannot trust a Tamil, a Hindu saint like Gurudev, what's the point in having a Tamil Eelam . . . Tamil homeland . . . Shame!' said Deepa.

The intelligence head laughed hysterically when one of his assistants quickly whipped out his pistol and pointed it at Deepa's head.

'Shoot me . . . shoot me . . . the world will call me a martyr,' she shouted.

Suddenly, Tamilselvan walked into the room, defused the situation and took her away.

I now wondered if the secret letter that Tamilselvan had written to Gurudev two years earlier was real and if Deepa had a hand in it. I asked Thambi if Deepa had ever told him of any letter that Tamilselvan had written to Gurudev.

He didn't seem to recollect her telling him something to that effect.

Looking around to see if any government officials or soldiers were coming, he whispered, 'She had also stolen some phone numbers from your phone . . . She also stole your Gurudev's phone number.'

Now I finally knew what she was doing with my phone in Jaffna. I thought to myself that perhaps she was the one who had given Gurudev's phone number to Nadesan, the LTTE political head who had called him from the battlefield asking him to facilitate 'a truce' a fortnight before the war ended.

As other inmates of the dormitory started trooping in, Thambi got a little nervous and took me out. He whispered that he would introduce me to an important person the next day and then walked away casually, as though he had absolutely nothing to do with me.

I was puzzled.

~

Next day, Thambi led me to a white tarpaulin tent. It was smelling due to the unwashed clothes dumped in a corner and a plate with half-consumed food that was buzzing with flies enjoying their banquet.

I was put off but this was a relief camp for internally displaced people and not a glamorous room.

There was a ruckus near the tent as some women were fighting next to the water tanker that came to deliver drinking water. I looked out to see the battle of the pots, as red, green and blue plastic clashed.

Inside the white tent, a blue tarpaulin sheet partially covered the mud floor. Thambi placed a rickety chair on it saying, 'I will call Anthony soon.'

As I waited curiously, a man with just one arm walked in. He seemed totally surprised to see me there. He asked if I was the counselling expert who was delivering the breathing technique classes. He settled on the floor and slowly began to chat me up.

I asked him if Thambi had told him to meet me. He replied in the negative and continued speaking. Here was a gatecrasher!

I had to get back to Vavuniya town, but still decided to hear him out.

Siva's family and twenty-four other relatives and friends were at the border of a quiet lagoon at 3 a.m. They had somehow reached there after negotiating plants and creepers along the way, crawling on the sand inch by inch and hiding from LTTE soldiers. There were ten children and eight women in the group.

His eight-year-old son was hungry. He hadn't eaten anything since breakfast the previous morning. The boy began to cry and ask for food but no one in the group had any food. Not wanting even a whisper to reach the dark skies, Siva's wife gagged the boy's mouth to silence him.

She picked a few leaves from a shrub nearby and slowly began to feed her son, asking him to chew them well. When he spat them out, she whispered into his ear that the leaves were all she had to feed him and that he had to eat them if he was really hungry. The boy chewed on the leaves reluctantly and cried quietly.

In a few minutes, they had crawled into the cool waters of the lagoon. Suddenly, the LTTE cadres opened fire. They thought that some of their cadres were trying to escape into the territory just beyond the lagoon, that the advancing Lankan army had won over a few days earlier.

Siva saw his uncle's head get shredded into pieces and blood spraying out of his neck, splashing his face, leaving it red. The children began to scream in fear even as the adults dragged them into the lagoon to continue with their great escape.

They had to make it to the other side, come hell or high water.

Siva's wife looked around for their son. Just then, the Lankan army began to fire from the opposite side, perhaps thinking that some LTTE cadres were trying to swim towards their side under the cover of darkness.

The next moment, she heard their son scream and sink.

She howled in agony as the water level rose and rushed to lift up her son's sunken body. Instead, her hands lifted out of the water an old woman's head. The moonlight spotlighted this horror, even as Siva dragged her and their daughter forward forcefully to continue crossing the lagoon.

The sand was sinking under their feet from time to time and the fish were nibbling at their feet. This made the crossing of the lagoon really slow. This was the same place where they often managed to get a handsome catch of fish and prawns for several years since their childhood.

Every few minutes they were forced to duck into the waters to escape the firing aimed at them from both sides. The air was foul due to the stench of dead bodies. Siva and the others tripped over some of them.

A bullet ripped his left arm completely. He collapsed into the water. A hefty cousin pulled Siva out of the water and wrapped a shirt around his arm to stop the blood. The cousin then carried him over his shoulders.

'Are we ever going to reach our destination?' mumbled Siva's friend when he saw another bullet slice through his newly married friend's head. The firing had left four others dead.

About an hour later, they were nearly blinded due to a powerful torchlight. They heard Sinhalese.

On reaching the shore, a Lankan soldier loudly ordered them to raise their hands high up, fearing that any one of them could be a suicide bomber.

After a thorough body search, they were offered some biscuits and drinking water. Just Siva and a few others had managed to make it. His daughter was now missing.

The army men put them on a waiting bus with some more refugees who had crossed the lagoon a few days earlier. As soon as the bus reached the Vavuniya camp, Siva was rushed to the town hospital for surgery.

Wiping the sweat off his forehead, Siva now told me, 'If not for my wife, I would have taken my life already.' He did not want her to be left alone and scarred due to the loss of her entire family.

I wondered if Tamil aspirations now stood drowned, leaving a whole generation of people marooned.

His titanic sorrow outweighed his chivalrous demeanour and I began to counsel him.

Siva thanked me and walked out after a few minutes, leaving me wondering about the trials and tribulations of life.

~

Shortly after Siva's departure, Thambi rushed in with Anthony, a ruggedly confident man in his mid-thirties, with biceps bursting through his yellow shirt. I would have cast him in a movie if I were in the film industry.

He gave me a half-smile and settled on the floor. 'Vavuniya is also our Tamil motherland, so I am comfortable wherever I sit,' he told me in his opening remarks. Thambi left the tent.

'By telling you this information, I don't expect any favour from you. I am a fighter. Strong fighter,' he said bluntly.

He told me that his friend was tortured the previous week, hung upside down and a few of his fingernails were ripped off by the intelligence agency people. They suspected his involvement in the assassination of a Lankan minister.

I told Anthony to share freely and without hesitation whatever he wanted to tell me. I gently encouraged him to speak out.

He revealed that he was the security guard at one of the underground bunkers in Kilinochchi for almost a week, when the LTTE intelligence chief and his trusted aide were finalizing details of the modus operandi to kidnap Gurudev. This happened over two straight meetings.

They had code-named the kidnap plan 'Bunker 21' to denote 21 September after the International Day of Peace and the day Gurudev was to meet with Prabhakaran in 2006. Three bunkers were already prepared for Gurudev so that he could be shifted every two days to avoid detection by satellite.

A few sets of white dhotis (traditional wear in the Indian subcontinent) and shirts had already been purchased from Colombo for Gurudev's use. The LTTE had gathered every single detail about him, even the food he liked. Their intelligence wing was well-trained in gathering and processing even classified information, reiterated Anthony.

Suddenly, I spotted a snake sneaking into the tent and rushed out, but Anthony was still inside. I peeped in, only to see him catch the snake with ease and give it a farewell.

Just then, a passing soldier asked me, 'You are still here? Your stress relief class is not yet over?'

I replied, 'A man wants extra classes . . . Counselling for depression.'

He smiled and walked away. In that month, the entire Sri Lankan security that was guarding these camps had become friendly with us, even learning a few breathing techniques as and when they found the time.

I walked back into the tent. Anthony told me that having lived in jungles since his childhood he knew how to handle even tigers! He laughed with a roar.

Anthony continued that the intelligence chief had then cautioned his aide, saying that Prabhakaran had explicitly instructed him that absolutely no harm, not even a scratch, should befall Gurudev.

'This sounds like a long-term plan to hold him captive. But why did they want to kidnap him?' I interjected.

The LTTE had planned to hold him in captivity for three months so that they could halt the incessant Sri Lankan bombings and fighting in the east.

This cooling-off period would have been a chance to smuggle in more arms, ammunition and fuel. A forcible recruitment drive was also in place in all LTTE-controlled areas to overcome the shortage of fighters.

'We had one of the most brilliant intelligence agents in the world,' Anthony boasted with pride, as he thumped his chest and went on to reveal that 'Indian response scenarios' to the kidnapping were also discussed.

He added that four more people knew of this plan and they were currently staying in the relief camp.

I jogged my memory back to the time when Swamiji spoke of the four people who were there when Gurudev had gone to meet Prabhakaran in Kilinochchi. I recollected him saying that they were running in and out of the room to make frantic calls.

I wondered if those calls were related to the plan to kidnap Gurudev.

I wish I had recorded this meeting with Anthony, but I didn't have my phone inside the camp as our phones were deposited with the security at the entrance of the massive refugee camp.

I asked Anthony if he could introduce me to those four people. He bluntly refused my request, as if he had somehow realized that too much had been revealed too soon.

The day Gurudev was in Kilinochchi, he was to be whisked away in a simple van, and the others who accompanied him were to be dropped off at the Kilinochchi checkpost to head back to Colombo.

I asked Anthony if he knew why the plan wasn't implemented at all. He shook his head and simply replied that he had no clue.

I retorted, 'You should have kidnapped Gurudev. What a mistake you people made.'

He was shocked and told me, 'How can you yourself say that?'

I stood wondering why the LTTE hadn't executed its plan. Anthony stood up puzzled. Scratching his head, he asked, 'I wonder if you are a double agent here.'

Perhaps with this kidnapping, Prabhakaran would have had the time and space to understand and know Gurudev much better.

What a missed chance!

~

A few weeks later, in October 2009, I made a secret trip to Kilinochchi and visited the 'tiger's den', the underground bunker where Prabhakaran had stayed for many years.

As I went down each floor, I wondered if this was the place where he had decided not to meet Gurudev or was it in the green conference room that they had plotted 'Bunker 21'.

The unknown often lies in the depths.

18

A Wish and Three Generations

A year after the culmination of the war, I began to tour various parts of the island to build consensus on Gurudev's Uniting Hearts and Minds initiative, which focused on promoting post-war reconciliation efforts and reaching out to various sections of both the Tamil and Sinhalese population. Gurudev had directed me to meet with educationists, religious leaders, lawmakers and prominent members of civil society.

In 2013, continuing this initiative, I happened to revisit one of my favourite spots in Sri Lanka.

I carried a large, gleaming plate full of neatly arranged lotus buds, both pink and white, to offer at the Kataragama temple. I was visiting the temple seven years after Gurudev's 2006 visit there.

For me, that temple was a common meeting ground for Tamils and Sinhalese Buddhists. A sacred space celebrated often, where both the communities meet, mingle and pray in harmony.

In a few days, I was going to say goodbye to the Lankan soil that I had survived on for nine years, though at times I felt as if I lived here for nine lifetimes!

I was seated on a concrete bench near the ancient temple when smoke from hundreds of incense sticks lit by the faithful wafted through the air. I recollected the helicopter trip we had undertaken in April 2009 while visiting the Vavuniya refugee camps. A little after we took off, Gurudev asked me for the diary that I had on my lap.

He flipped the pages and began to write something.

As I wondered what he was writing in it, I looked out of the tiny window to take in a glimpse of the light, sunny afternoon, not wanting him to take notice of my curiosity.

Our helicopter was cruising above a long highway with thick greens on either side. It felt like a journey to nowhere.

In a few minutes, he asked Tamitegama, our then secretary general of the Art of Living in the island, 'Where is Anuradhapura?'

Tami, as we addressed him lovingly, looked out of the window and replied, 'We are flying over it right now!'

Gurudev returned the diary after fifteen minutes and asked me to read it.

I was delighted to see his handwritten notes:

No more war. No more violence. Peace and prosperity for the people of Sri Lanka. Justice, dignity and equal rights for all. Homes and hope rebuilt.

Children must be given confidence and education. Youth must be empowered. Women and war widows island-wide must be given respect and empowered.

Every Tamil resettled in their homes. A new, bright, prosperous Sri Lanka with peaceful coexistence and harmony.

Gurudev had telegraphed his wishes and blessings for the Sri Lankan people.

The temple bells rang and I went in to offer prayers. I then came out to light nine lamps and incense sticks and sat near a huge, old banyan tree to meditate for a while.

In my reckoning, the war had wiped out almost an entire generation of people.

When I had first landed in Sri Lanka, I had met with several people from the 1940s, 1950s and earlier generations. Elders with longer memories recollected the good old days when everyone coexisted peacefully.

I worked closely with some second-generation Sri Lankans, most of whom had bought into the idea of war and violence, justifying it as a means to an end.

And just after the war concluded, I began to encounter an increasing number of a whole new generation. The third generation. One that just did not want a war any more.

In nine years, I had coexisted with three generations, almost simultaneously.

The Art of Living continued to rehabilitate hundreds of ex-LTTE cadres and war survivors, including war widows. Our work continues to this day.

I recollect some of the lessons I learned from Gurudev during my long journey in that island nation. It is imperative to take responsibility to foster peace by going beyond one's sense of duty. In doing your duty, you do what you have to do, but in taking responsibility, you go beyond your comfort zone.

I remember Gurudev saying that when your neighbour's house is on fire you don't keep waiting for an invitation to go and help.

And Gurudev did exactly that—he just stepped out to connect, help and assist his neighbouring islanders in every possible way.

That's one of the key things that simply makes one human and a humanitarian.

Secondly, in working with Gurudev, my personal experience is that you are not part of a celebrity status but a tradition of a full-time working master, a wisdom-smith and a relaxed enigma!

I couldn't have asked for a better 'boss' in this lifetime!

Finally, as he says, 'War is the worst act of reason.' One tries to make every justification, giving seemingly believable reasons, to conduct violence and war.

An army general once confronted a captain, 'You are a really capable man. Amazing guy. If only you stop drinking so much and remain sober, you can rise to become a colonel.'

The captain replied, 'Sir, while I am drunk, I am already a general but when I am sober, I will still be just a colonel. It is better I enjoy being a general when I am drunk.'

Any reason is enough to create and live in an illusion.

As I write this chapter, the breaking news is that the Taliban has taken control of Afghanistan. Twenty years of war, billions of dollars spent, hundreds of deaths, the sacrifice of thousands of soldiers from several Western countries seem to have evaporated in thin air, in just a few weeks. Do we need a bigger illusion?

Whether it's the war on environment or climate, fanaticism, terror or biowarfare, conflict at home or in the mind, I personally believe that the world needs more peacemakers now than ever before. It is the responsibility of the youth of the world to play this role in their society and community, wherever they are and in whatever capacity they can.

Yes, we still need thousands of peacemakers to take the message of non-violence and peace to the future generations.

~

During my December 2013 flight back to India, the pilot announced, 'Ladies and gentlemen. This is your captain here . . . on the right side, you can see the Ram Setu bridge. It's a low tide today. Enjoy the view.'

As I looked down to take one last look at the Ram Setu bridge, I was overwhelmed by how this ancient and beautiful bridge stood there, strong, for centuries, quietly witnessing the tides, low or high, watching every storm and wave come and go in that country.

Though the war was won, is there peace?

Pause for a Moment Here!

Dedicate your tribute to all those who died, served in or survived the twenty-six-year war in Sri Lanka. You may express yourself with a poem, a sketch, words of gratitude or comfort, a comment or just leave your signature here. It's your page.

List of Sources

- BBC, 'Sri Lanka Profile—Timeline', 18 November 2019, https://www.bbc.com/news/world-south-asia-12004081.
- Jayshree Bajoria, 'The Sri Lankan Conflict', Council on Foreign Relations, 18 May 2009, https://www.cfr.org/backgrounder/sri-lankan-conflict.
- UN Peacemaker, 'Bandaranaike–Chelvanayakam Pact, 26 July 1957', Sri Lanka Secretariat for Coordinating the Peace Process (SCOPP), https://peacemaker.un.org/sites/peacemaker.un.org/files/LK_570726_Bandranayaki%20Chelvanayakam%20Pact.pdf.
- Tamil Guardian, 'Root causes of the ethnic conflict in Sri Lanka', 19 February 2008, https://www.tamilguardian.com/content/root-causes-ethnic-conflict-sri-lanka.
- A. Jeyaratnam Wilson, *The Break-up of Sri Lanka: The Sinhalese-Tamil Conflict*, Hurst Publishers, 1988, p 131.
- IRIN, 'Sri Lanka: Remembering the riots that triggered 25 years of conflict', 25 July 2008, available at: https://www.refworld.org/docid/488f17e613.html.
- BBC, 'Remembering Sri Lanka's Black July', 23 July 2013, https://www.bbc.com/news/world-asia-23402727.
- Eelam View, 'Leader V Prabhakaran's Hero day speech 1992–2008 English translation', 11 November 2012, https://www.eelamview.com/2012/11/11/leader-v-prabakarans-heros-day-speech-1992-2008-english-translation/.
- UN Peacemaker, 'Agreement on a Ceasefire between the Government of the Democratic Socialist Republic of Sri Lanka and the Liberation Tigers of Tamil Eelam', 22 February 2002, https://peacemaker.un.org/sites/peacemaker.un.org/files/LK_020222_CeasefireAgreementGovernment-LiberationTigersTamilEelam.pdf.
- D.K. Hari and D.K. Hema Hari, *Ramayana in Lanka*, Sri Sri Publications Trust, 2010, pp. 48–49.

- Gurudev Sri Sri Ravi Shankar, *An Intimate Note to the Sincere Seeker*, Sri Sri Publications Trust, 2008, second edition July 2021.
- Charu Lata Joshi, 'No Other Agency except the LTTE Was Involved: D.R. Karthikeyan', *India Today*, 1 June 2013, https://www.indiatoday.in/magazine/interview/story/19960531-no-other-agency-except-the-ltte-was-involved-d-r-karthikeyan-833001-1996-05-31.
- Gurudev Sri Sri Ravi Shankar, 'Sri Sri Invited to Signing of FARC-Colombian Government Peace Agreement', 24 September 2016, https://www.srisriravishankar.org/work/peace-initiatives/sri-sri-invited-farc-colombia-peace-signing.
- D. Balasubramanian, 'In Search of the Sanjeevani Plant of Ramayana', *The Hindu*, 16 December 2016, https://www.thehindu.com/sci-tech/science/In-search-of-the-Sanjeevani-plant-of-Ramayana/article16880681.ece.
- Valmiki, Valmiki Ramayana (Book VI : Yuddha Kanda—Book of War, Chapter [Sarga] 74, Sanskrit documents), https://sanskritdocuments.org/sites/valmikiramayan/yuddha/sarga74/yuddha_74_frame.htm.
- Gurudev Sri Sri Ravi Shankar, 'Manipur CM Lauds Gurudev Sri Sri Ravi Shankar after 68 Militants Surrender', 23 September 2017, https://www.srisriravishankar.org/work/peace-initiatives/manipur-cm-lauds-gurudev-sri-sri-ravi-shankar-68-militants-surrender.
- South Asian Analysis Group, 'Sri Lanka: Mavil Aru Operation & After—An Analysis', 12 August 2006, https://web.archive.org/web/20100620203142/http:/southasiaanalysis.org/papers20/paper1908.html.
- Republic World, 'Sri Sri Ravi Shankar Speaks to Arnab on His Mediation's Role in Ayodhya Solution', 22 September 2021, https://www.republicworld.com/india-news/general-news/sri-sri-ravi-shankar-speaks-to-arnab-on-his-mediations-role-in-ayodhya-solution.html.

- Tamil Guardian, 'Remembering the Sencholai massacre 14 years on', 13 August 2020, https://www.tamilguardian.com/content/remembering-sencholai-massacre-14-years.
- Refworld, 'Refugee Review Tribunal Australia, RRT Research Response', 19 September 2008, refworld.org/pdfid/4b6fe29bd.pdf.
- Canada: Immigration and Refugee Board of Canada, 'Sri Lanka: Information on checkpoints in Vavuniya', 1 February 1993, LKA13149, available at: https://www.refworld.org/docid/3ae6ab6454.html.
- T. Ramakrishnan, 'T.N. Seshan (1932–2019) | The man who cleaned up the Indian electoral system', *The Hindu*, 11 November 2019, https://www.thehindu.com/news/national/tn-seshan-obituary-the-man-who-cleaned-up-the-indian-electoral-system/article29939660.ece.
- UN High Commissioner for Refugees (UNHCR), 'UNHCR CDR Background Paper on Refugees and Asylum Seekers from Sri Lanka', 1 March 1997, available at: https://www.refworld.org/docid/3ae6a6470.html.
- Outlook India, 'No Other Option But An Independent State . . .', 26 November 2006, https://www.outlookindia.com/website/story/no-other-option-but-an-independent-state/233232.
- UN Peacemaker, 'Indo-Lanka Accord, Colombo, 29 July 1987', https://peacemaker.un.org/sites/peacemaker.un.org/files/IN LK_870729_Indo-Lanka Accord.pdf.
- M. Concelia Mariampillai, *The Spirit Blows Where It Wills*, Sri Sri Publications Trust, 2014.
- The Gazette of India, 'The Citizenship Amendment (Act), 2019', 12 December 2019, https://www.egazette.nic.in/WriteReadData/2019/214646.pdf.
- Cricketnext Staff, 'On This Day - March 3, 2009: A Dark Day for International Cricket as Sri Lankan Cricketers Attacked by Terrorists', *News18*, 3 March 2021, https://www.news18.com/cricketnext/news/on-this-day-march-3-2009-a-dark-day-

for-international-cricket-as-sri-lankan-cricketers-attacked-by-terrorists-3492977.html.

- UN News, 'Sri Lanka: Actions by Government Forces, Rebels Possible War Crimes—UN Rights Chief', 13 March 2009, https://news.un.org/en/story/2009/03/293862.

- TNN, 'Jaya's Poll Vault: 'Tamil Eelam' Only Way out', *The Times of India*, https://timesofindia.indiatimes.com/india/jayas-poll-vault-tamil-eelam-only-way-out/articleshow/4449288.cms.

- Charles Petrie, UN Secretary-General and, UN Internal Review Panel on United Nations Action in Sri Lanka, 'Report of the Secretary-General's Internal Review Panel on United Nations Action in Sri Lanka', November 2012, https://digitallibrary.un.org/record/737299?ln=en.

- 'LTTE Top Guns' Death Still a Mystery', *Hindustan Times*, 21 May 2009, http://www.hindustantimes.com/world/ltte-top-guns-death-still-a-mystery/story-6MZSh8qiDfDt2BH7RjOcaN.html.

- Mail Today, 'Tiger Leaders Killed While Surrendering', *India Today*, 26 May 2009, https://www.indiatoday.in/headlines-today-top-stories/story/tiger-leaders-killed-while-surrendering-48629-2009-05-26

- UN News, 'UN Chief "Appalled" by Weekend Death Toll in Sri Lankan Conflict', 11 May 2009, https://news.un.org/en/story/2009/05/299612.

- 'Sri Lankan Situation like a Human Tsunami: Sri Ravi Shankar', *Hindustan Times*, 26 April 2009, https://www.hindustantimes.com/world/sri-lankan-situation-like-a-human-tsunami-sri-ravi-shankar/story-S2QeffYnsj1mIJaU6NwjfO.html.

- IANS, 'LTTE Asks Ravi Shankar to Facilitate Ceasefire', *India Today*, 4 May 2009, https://www.indiatoday.in/headlines-today-top-stories/story/ltte-asks-ravi-shankar-to-facilitate-ceasefire-46534-2009-05-04

- 'LTTE Asks Ravi Shankar to Facilitate Ceasefire', *Hindustan Times*, 4 May 2009, https://www.hindustantimes.com/india/ltte-asks-ravi-shankar-to-facilitate-ceasefire/story-8FFkU5UXob7pNScraXde3H.html

- 'LTTE Asks Ravi Shankar to Facilitate Ceasefire', *New Indian Express*, 15 May 2012, https://www.newindianexpress.com/world/2009/may/04/ltte-asks-ravi-shankar-to-facilitate-ceasefire-46449.html